Communicating with Your Dog

A Humane Approach to Dog Training

by Ted Baer

With photographs by the author
and other renowned dog photographers

Dedication

To Mom and Dad for their
constant encouragement throughout
my life. I owe them a debt too
large to ever repay.

All inquiries should be addressed to:
Barron's Educational Series, Inc.
250 Wireless Boulevard
Hauppauge, New York 11788

http://www.barronseduc.com

Library of Congress Catalog Card No. 98-43583

International Standard Book No. 0-7641-0758-5

Library of Congress Cataloging-in-Publication Data

Baer, Ted.
    Communicating with your dog ; twenty magic words /
Ted Baer. — 2nd ed.
      p.   cm.
    Includes index.
    ISBN 0-7641-0758-5
    1. Dogs—Training. 2. Dogs—Behavior. 3. Human-animal
communication. I. Title.
SF431.B3225   1999
636.7'088'7—dc21   98-43583
                                     CIP

Printed in Hong Kong

987654321

Photo Credits

    Tara Darling: pages viii, 20, 55, 70, 96, 97, 152, 154,
162, 163; Kent and Donna Dannen: pages ix, 17, 24 left, 48,
141; Norvia Behling: title page and pages 2, 12, 15, 22, 24
right, 40, 42, 58, 66, 102, 128,134, 148,155; Sharon Eide:
pages 3, 26, 36, 56, 58, 84, 110, 135, 147, 160, 165; Bonnie
Nance: page 4; Elizabeth Flynn: pages 7, 11, 74, 100;
Judith E. Strom: pages 68, 94, 99, 150, 151; Daniel
Johnson: page 103; Jan Mahood, page 106; Toni Tucker:
page 108, 159; Winter Churchill: page 138; Paola Visintini:
page 158. All other photos and cover photos by the author.

The Author

    Ted Baer has worked in the motion picture industry as a
dog trainer. His dog, Tundra, has performed in television,
commercials, and full-length films. She won the coveted
PATSY, the American Humane Association's highest award
for a performing animal. Ted is also a canine counselor and
author of *How to Teach Your Old Dog New Tricks,* pub-
lished by Barron's.

Important Note

    This book tells the reader how to train his or her dog.
The author and the publisher consider it important to
point out that the advice given in this book is meant primarily for normally developed and socialized dogs of
good health and temperament.

    Anyone attempting to train an adult dog, especially
one that the owner has adopted as an adult, should be
aware that the animal has already formed its basic
impressions of human beings. The new owner should
watch the animal carefully, including its behavior toward
humans, and should meet the previous owner, if possible. If the dog comes from a shelter, it may be possible
to get some information on the dog's background and
behavior there. There are dogs that, as a result of bad
experiences with humans, behave in an unpredictable
manner, or might even bite. Only experienced owners
who have trained such dogs should consider adopting
them.

    Caution is further advised in socializing dogs with
other dogs or with children and in exercising the dog
without a leash.

    Even well-behaved and carefully supervised dogs
sometimes damage someone else's property or cause
accidents. It is therefore in the owner's interest to be
adequately insured against such eventualities, and we
strongly urge every dog owner to purchase a liability
policy that covers the dog.

    Finally, we advise all owners to be aware of local and
state dog-related laws and regulations.

Contents

Introduction   vi

1.   **Communication By Means of a Language**   1

2.   **Family Cooperation**   5

3.   **Communication Bell**   9

4.   **The Rules**   13
     Be Consistent   13
     Work as a Family Unit   13
     Match Voice Tone to Command   14
     Exercise Patience   14
     Think Like a Dog   15
     Respect Your Dog as a "Person"   16
     Praise Rather Than Punish   16
     Praise or Correct Immediately   19
     Ask Only the Possible   19
     Give a Command Only Once   19
     Release Each Command   20
     Allow Your Dog to Be Good   20
     Train Before Dinner   21
     Play After Other Training Sessions   21
     Record Your Dog's Progress   22

5.   **Your Dog's First Word**   23

6.   **Feedback Words—*Good*, *Bad*, and *No***   25

7.   **Major Directives—*Stay*, *Go*, and *Come***   27

8.   **Body Positions—*Sit* and *Down***   37

9. Secondary Commands—*Hold*, *Get*, *Drop*, *Bring*, *Up*, and *Nose*   43

10. Special Commands—*Look*, *Bark*, *Walk*, *Okay*, and *Hurry*   59

11. A Quiz   69

12. Hand Signals   75
    The Handclap   75
    The Directed *Go*   76
    The Directed *Come*   78
    The *Down*   81
    The *Stay*   84

13. Taking the Language a Few Steps Farther   85
    Categories of New Words   85
    The Word *Back*   91
    The Word *Catch*   92
    The Word *Eat*   93
    The Word *Heel*   93
    The Word *Jump*   95
    The Word *Pull*   96
    The Words *Upstairs* and *Downstairs*   96
    The Word *Stand*   98
    The Word *Take*   98
    The Command *Watch It!*   99

14. House-training—A Necessity   101
    Already House-trained? Skip this Chapter!   101
    When You Are Home   102
    While You Are Sleeping   104
    Leaving Your Dog Home Alone   107

15. The Problem Child   111
    Use of the Squirt Bottle   112
    The Backyard Barker   112
    The Chewer   114
    The Trash Examiner   115
    The Body Climber   117
    The Wallflower   118
    The Hyperactive Hound   120
    The Thief   121

The Grabber   122
The Digger   123
The Biter   124
The Prizefighter   126
The Chaser   128
The Backyard Surpriser   129
The Occasional Accident-er   130
The Macho Scenter   131
The Bitch in Heat   132
Minor Bad Habits   134

16. The Problem Parent   **137**
Unidentified Dog   137
The Pickup Rider   139
The Wanderer   140
Junk Food Junkie   142
The Shaggy Dog   143
Unpedicured Pooch   144
The Toilet Drinker   146

17. Doggie I.Q. Tests   **149**
Choosing a Dog   149
Quick Shopping Tips   151
Tips for the Very Committed   152
Senses Tests   155
Aptitude Tests   156
Observation Tests   158
Ongoing Tests   158

18. Parting Words   **161**

Index   **166**

Introduction

The manuscript for this book, like most, was rejected by publisher after publisher. I had devised a simple communication system that would work well with any dog. This system allowed me to teach my dog, Tundra, an extensive vocabulary of commands, allowing her to perform amazing behaviors. She won the highest award a dog can win in the Television and Motion Picture Industry, the P.A.T.S.Y. Award, for her first national performance when she appeared on the "Love Boat." The American Humane Association gave Tundra the only award it gave a performing canine that year. And yet I couldn't interest a publisher in my new system. There were just too many dog training books on the market. Barron's took a chance with me, and that year *Communicating with Your Dog* received a Dog Writers' Association of America Award. It was a dream come true!

You can imagine my delight when my publisher told me that, because of the book's commercial success, we would be doing a Second Edition. Although I had received wonderful reviews from book critics, some had mentioned topics in the book that were missing or could be improved. Readers had also written letters requesting additional advice. I jumped at the chance to rework the book, incorporating topics that had not previously been covered. I think you'll find that *Communicating with Your Dog* is the only dog training book you'll ever need. I not only outline a simple communication system for you to share with your dog, but I've added valuable information on initial house training, testing your dog's I.Q., and choosing the right dog. Additionally, I've adopted a gentler, more motivational approach to solving behavior problems. You'll find my book simple and fun!

The mixture of instincts and training can make for a winning combination.

The development of a communication system for use with dogs is long overdue. Through the course of history, people have developed intricate languages to communicate with each other and even with machines. At their side through this struggle was the dog. Different breeds were developed for their respective skills. These instinctive skills of herding, guarding, hunting, sled pulling, and even rescuing helped people accomplish their goals. Though the need for a simple and logical dog language was evident, no such language had been developed.

In this book I will teach you to communicate with your dog through an easy-to-learn twenty-word language. You will learn simple training skills for teaching the language to your dog. This will serve as a basis for further training and will reward both of you with greater friendship and understanding.

DOG PSYCHOLOG
The ... of Dog Traini...

Chapter 1

Communication By Means of a Language

Dogs can be proud of the old adage associated with them. The phrase "man's best friend" tells us a lot about the history of dogs and their basic nature. I cannot think of a better compliment or a truer characterization of dogs in general.

Fido's only aim is to please you. You are the highlight of his life. He studies you and depends on you for his food, water, and shelter. He recognizes how you hold your body when you're happy, angry, nervous, or tired. He can even sense your deep feelings. Gradually, Fido will adopt your character, personality, and, some believe, even your looks.

The next time you find yourself in a bad mood, observe the way your dog behaves. The typical dog senses your mood and, with ears back, will approach you submissively, as if to apologize for not pleasing you.

Dogs are loyal companions whose lack of understanding is not their fault. Relatively few dogs who get scolded or punished ever know why. Dogs need to be disciplined in a way that enables them to understand what they did wrong. If Fido doesn't do what he's told, chances are that you are at fault.

To give your dog a chance to please you, it is necessary that you use a system of communication that is simple and clear. Though people possess intelligence, reason, logic, and, for the most part, wisdom, they speak to their dogs in a confusing and illogical way.

The widely used commands, "Sit down!" and "Lie down!" are good examples of this. Notice that both commands use two words when only one is necessary. Also, in each of the commands you find the word "down." Does the confusion end here? Not quite. When using the "lie down" command, people often interchange "lie" and "lay." Fido's life would be much simpler if "sit" were used for sitting and "down" for lying down.

Fido will often carry out a master's command, but not because the command is stated correctly. Take the case when the resident chef

At last count, Tundra had a vocabulary of more than two hundred words.

1

When this Labrador Retriever puppy grows up, she'll be able to steal food from the table, so it's important to teach her good manners now.

catches his or her best friend in the kitchen trying to make off with the family's lamb chops and yells, "You rotten dog! Get out of here!" Fido makes tracks and hides for a while—not because he understands the words of the command, but because he senses his master's displeasure.

The best dog trainers in the world have said that a dog is capable of learning as many as one hundred verbal commands in a lifetime. My star pupil, Tundra, knows more than two hundred verbal commands and more than seventy hand signals. Tundra's vocabulary has grown to this level quickly and forms a very solid base. With this

base I am now able to communicate any action to her verbally. New words are added only occasionally, when needed.

In regard to Tundra's training, I would like to point out that her knowledge increased at an accelerating rate. In other words, as Tundra's knowledge developed, things came to her more quickly and easily. Few researchers have been concerned with the rate at which a dog learns. But it seems logical that it would be much easier for Tundra to relate any new training to that which she already knew and understood—and so it was. Based on my experience, I do not believe there is a saturation point in a dog's learning ability.

The special language found in this book will allow your dog to grow in its ability to understand communications. You will be given twenty words and, with consistent use and reinforcement, your pet will develop a "vocabulary," much as a young child does. The consistency in using the same words, the same method of speaking, and the same logical word order will avoid confusion. Your success at using this language will determine your dog's success in understanding your wishes.

Originally, when teaching Tundra the word "growl," a problem arose because its sound was too close to the command "howl." The word command "growl" was changed to "scare," and I no longer confused her. To avoid this kind of confusion and to make it easier for your dog, the "magic" words used in this book are one-syllable words, each with its own separate and identifiable sound.

It's a wonderful feeling owning a dog that listens to you. You'll find that the twenty-word language will give you a solid base for communication. Your dog will be a happy dog. It will not only know when it has been bad or good, but it will understand your wishes and be able to please you more. Because of its new knowledge, you'll be more likely to take your best friend with you wherever you go. So please be selfish and spoil yourself. Spend a little time with your dog. It's the only investment that I know of that returns a hundredfold.

Chapter 2
Family Cooperation

It is extremely important that you have your family's cooperation in carrying out the program presented in this book. Review the material and practice it daily with your dog. Make sure that your family understands what you are trying to do and is willing to help. Assure them that the program is simple and easy if carried out properly. Explain to them the value of having a dog that follows simple commands.

When I say "family," I mean everyone who comes in contact with your dog in your house. That includes all members of the household and frequent visitors—at least those visitors who like to talk and play with your dog.

It will be easy to gain your family's cooperation if you go about it in the right way. Start by arousing their interest. Pick a time to introduce and discuss the program when the family normally gathers together. You can't expect them all to take the time to read this book. Tell them the purpose of a special dog language. Stress how easy it will be for them to learn twenty words in particular sequences.

Next, discuss each of the rules found in Chapter 4. As you bring up each one, allow your family to discuss what it means and why it is important. Make certain that they understand each of the rules.

Finally, introduce the first nine words of the language to your family. These words will be found in Chapters 5, 6, 7, and 8. Go over each individually. Explain the word's meaning and talk about its uses. Members of the family will be allowed to use only these nine words when talking to your dog.

Included in this chapter, you will find an outline that you may want to

Consistency is the key to effective teaching. If everyone in the family uses only the correct words, your dog's progress will be accelerated.

Meeting Outline

The Purpose of a Special Dog Language

1. Effective communication makes life easier for your dog and makes him or her happy and obedient.
2. The twenty-word language is simple and logical for your dog.
3. Anything else is confusing.
4. Consistent use of the words avoids confusion.
5. Lack of understanding is not your dog's fault.
6. The family will find it simple, beneficial, educational, and fun.

The Rules

1. Be consistent.
2. Work as a family unit.
3. Match voice tone to command.
4. Exercise patience.
5. Think like a dog.
6. Respect your dog as a "person."
7. Praise rather than punish.
8. Praise or correct immediately.
9. Ask only the possible.
10. Give a command only once.
11. Release each command.
12. Allow your dog to be good.
13. Train before dinner.
14. Play after other training sessions.
15. Record your dog's progress.

The First Nine Words

1. Your dog's name
2. *Good*
3. *Bad*
4. *No*
5. *Stay*
6. *Go*
7. *Come*
8. *Sit*
9. *Down*

Other Information

1. Only the nine words may be used by others.
2. "Gumball" can be used to reprimand a violator.
3. Respect each other's commands.
4. The rules and the commands will be posted.

follow at your family meeting. It contains the list of rules and commands that you will want to post for them. Place them where they can be referred to easily. If there are children in the family, you will want to post the rules and commands where they won't need an extension ladder to read them.

You must be a firm leader. The whole ball game depends upon you. You are the coach of your team, the captain, the umpire, the cheerleader, as well as one of the players.

As the coach it is up to you to review periodically the rules of the game with the team. As you introduce each new word, you must tell team members how you taught it and when it can be used.

As the captain you will inspire your teammates, you won't let them become discouraged, and you will keep them all working together. You will be the one calling the plays.

As the umpire you will correct any player who fails to follow the rules. Mistakes are inevitable. Catch them and correct them immediately. In doing this, I strongly recommend that you use a code word like "gumball" to let a player know that he or she has committed an error. As umpire it is up to you to see that no member of the team changes, repeats, or countermands another teammate's command. I will warn you about these things again in Chapter 4, and I'll tell you why they are mistakes.

As cheerleader you will keep the team enthusiastic. You have a product to get them excited about— Twenty Magic Words! Encourage your teammates when they need it. Support them in every way possible as they learn to communicate with their little mascot!

Always remember that you play the most important role in the game. The game is literally in your hands. Everything depends upon you. You will have to determine when the additional words will be introduced to your family. As with the initial words, you should teach them to your dog first. Chapter 10 has special commands that can be very helpful to the family. Review your family's progress and introduce new words at any convenient family gathering.

The benefits of the training program go far beyond the development of a lovable, obedient dog that truly can become a welcomed member of the family. You and the other members will become conscious of communication skills that you can apply not only to your dog but to little children and people in general. And the fact that you are working together on the project will bring you all closer together as a family.

Chapter 3
Communication Bell

Domesticated dogs have four major needs: food, water, expulsion of waste, and affection. Dogs have always struggled to communicate these needs.

When Fido is hungry he might be extremely friendly or look at you with a pair of sad eyes. When he is thirsty, he might make gestures toward the kitchen sink to get your attention, or even run around to the bathrooms to see if anyone left the lid of the toilet up. When he needs a walk to urinate or defecate, he will try anything from crying at the door to jumping up and down excitedly. As for affection, every owner knows the cute things that a dog will do to get some loving. Trying to read a newspaper in our house is always a challenge. That seems to be the signal for our dogs to stick their heads underneath it. We laugh each time, thnking it's cute and give them attention. Make sure you recognize and satisfy your dog's needs.

Of the four major needs, there are two, water and expulsion of waste, that Fido can easily warn you about. I credit a classmate from Rochester, New York, Chris Pond, for the following idea. (Others might have had and used the idea before him, but as of this writing, I have not seen the concept in print.) Chris's mother had a cat that used to play with her wind chimes. The cat would use the chimes to gain her attention when she wanted to go outside. When Chris got a dog, he started teaching him to play with the chimes. He said it came naturally to the dog after watching the cat do it many times. This idea deserves our attention and applause!

To begin using this idea in your own home, you need a bell. Any bell will work. If you have two dogs and one is small and the other large, choose a multiple bell design. Here the difference in size won't hinder the dogs from nudging the bell. Just hang the bell from your door knob with strong cord or maybe a leather strap. Each dog will choose to nudge it differently. Tundra noses it, while another member of our canine family has developed her own technique. She brushes against it with her body. One bell should be

Tundra noses the communication bell to tell us that she needs to be walked.

A well-designed multiple bell. The leather strap provides some protection for the door.

placed at the door where the dog normally leaves to go outside and another where he receives his water.

Training your dog to use the bell is an easy process. The secret is to be consistent! Every time Fido goes through the door for a walk, make him nudge the bell first. If he is standing over an empty water dish (heaven knows it was unintentional!) looking up for water, help him nudge the bell, and then give him the water.

To get your dog to nudge the bell, always use the same words: *nose* it. (see Chapter 9). Bring Fido's nose over to the bell, and help him to push it. When he finally sounds the bell, offer praise. Immediately take him for a walk or give him the water he wants. Refrain from ever giving your dog food for pushing the bell. Though food makes an excellent reward, it will always stick in the dog's mind that the bell means food. Be patient. The ten seconds that you devote to the bell four times a day will produce the results you want. Fido

Some dogs will brush against the bell to ring it.

might take from one week to two months to understand the bell, but then the bell will be part of his life.

If you find that your dog shies away from the bell, rub a favorite odor on it or tape a piece of food to it. Try a piece of roast beef. I guarantee that your dog will then be interested and will get close enough to it to nudge it with your help.

For the sake of your door, never allow Fido to paw the bell. The nails of his paws will not only scratch the door, but any other door in the house will also fall victim when Fido wants to get through. If you see Fido attempting to paw the bell, run over quickly, give him one squirt from a squirt bottle filled with water, and tell him sternly that he's bad (see Chapter 6). Then get to a positive note. Quickly help him to nose the bell, and give the just reward he deserves—water or a walk.

It will be a happy day the first time that Fido needs a walk and rings the bell on his own. Be sure to respond with praise, and then go for a walk immediately. Once your dog has mastered the communication bell, praise will no longer be necessary. Your dog will understand which bell to nose to get the message across, thus satisfying its need.

Chapter 4
The Rules

This chapter discusses the rules that you and your family should follow in teaching your dog the Twenty Magic Words. The rules set forth a basic guide to having an obedient dog. Review these rules occasionally to evaluate your progress. Any violation of these rules will hamper your progress with your dog.

Rule 1: Be Consistent

It is important that you be consistent in the use of the language. The dog who responds to "Fang, come!" will surely be confused if you say, "Get over here!" If you are using the wrong word to represent a particular action, the dog can't second-guess you. Use only the language outlined in this book.

You also must be consistent in your training methods. A consistent and proper correction is essential! If you are busy watching television and allow your dog to get away with something bad, your dog will certainly test you further. Often a person makes the mistake of praising a dog for incorrect behavior. An example of this is when Duchess jumps up on her owner. The owner's natural response is to pet the dog. In so doing, he or she rewards the dog for doing something objectionable.

Another good example is when Duchess is barking in the backyard—something dogs often do to gain attention. Not wanting to catch grief from the neighbors, the owner runs to the back door and offers her a silencing chew toy or even lets her come into the house. By rewarding the dog for barking, the owner simply defeats his or her own purpose. Such mistakes can make you your dog's pet.

Rule 2: Work as a Family Unit

The ideal way to train Duchess is to live alone with her. In general, the more people living with your dog, the harder it will be for you to train her. The only exception to this is when a family is operating as a

If you praise your dog when it responds to the Come command, it will be eager to obey the command again.

unit. The whole family must participate in your dog's language, discipline, rules, and, most importantly, her praise!

You have the responsibility of teaching your family the language and the rules. In Chapter 2, I discussed the need for family unity in training your dog. Before you begin teaching anyone else, however, be sure you have read this book from cover to cover and that you have a firm grasp of the material contained in the more pertinent sections.

Rule 3: Match Voice Tone to Command

Dogs rely on the tone of a person's voice. It is an easy guide they learn at an early age. A person's tone varies when he or she is angry, sad, happy, confused, or anxious. This acquired knowledge that your dog has learned can be helpful during training. Your tone should be in keeping with the nature of the command. In general, a command should sound serious. Your dog will be more likely to respect a command if it is given in a way that sounds important and urgent. *Good, bad,* and *no* (Chapter 6) need special attention given to the tone. These words are feedback words for your dog. Let Duchess feel from your tone whether she's been good or bad. On certain commands, an excited tone will stimulate excitement in

your dog. Play this by ear and watch for the reaction.

Volume is another variable in your voice that must be considered. I recommend a normal volume with the emphasis on tone. If your dog is some distance away, it will be necessary to increase your volume accordingly. Also, when you are upset with your dog, it is a good release of tension to yell "Bad!" using your full volume. Warning! Rumors may fly around your neighborhood as to your mental stability. Yell at your own risk!

During your training sessions, when your dog's attention is focused on you, it is a good idea to practice volume reduction. By giving your commands in a whisper, you will teach your dog to listen to you more closely.

Rule 4: Exercise Patience

We all have patience to a greater or lesser degree. The more you have, the more success you'll have in training your dog. Some people with little patience may still be successful with their dogs because of their great love for the four-legged beasties! When their patience runs out, these people should retreat, calm down, and then try again!

People say that I am very patient. Though I don't consider myself patient, I do enjoy teaching and playing with my dogs. I receive

more positive feedback from my dogs, and from people who see them, than from any other thing I've ever done. I derive pleasure from my animals. Remember that the fault is yours when Duchess doesn't do what she has been told. Be calm and closely examine how you confused her. Your dog loves you and wants to please you. Be patient.

Rule 5: Think Like a Dog

Human beings have been gifted with a complex brain and the ability to reason. In 1828, when Noah Webster compiled his famous dictionary, he collected 70,000 words in the English language. Most children understand hundreds of words by the age of two. Dogs, on the other hand, have smaller and less complex brains. They lack the logic and reasoning that allow humans to master information quickly. The number of words a bright dog understands is small. However, your dog is capable of learning many words that will close the communication gap. Duchess's progress is limited only to your ability and time. Teaching her the twenty-word language you will learn in this book is similar to programming a small computer in her brain. Later, when you command her by using a word or set of words, her response will follow automatically.

In order to accomplish this, it is necessary that you think like a dog. Duchess can't think on your level. You possess the reasoning and superior intelligence to bridge the gap. Identify her confusion. It may be caused by hearing a word that rhymes with another word, or seeing a hand signal that is poorly fed into her "computer." There might be distractions that affect your dog's performance. Distractions such as sounds, scents, people, and other animals can make it hard for Duchess to concentrate on you and your command. If you think like a dog and talk to her on her own level, you'll be a happy dog owner!

Rule 6: Respect Your Dog as a "Person"

Treat your dog as you would treat another person you might meet. When you walk through your front door and greet the family, give a short burst of attention to Duchess, too. If you find her too excited when she sees you, make her sit and give her a scratch on the head. Then be sure to release her from the *sit* command. Always be happy to see your dog when a separation has occurred, and let her know it. It's not only polite, but you'll find your dog will love you even more.

Rule 7: Praise Rather Than Punish

Stress the positive, lightly touch on the negative, and turn that negative into a positive. It's simple! Encourage the things you want your dog to do, and discourage the *bad* habits.

The idea of turning a negative into a positive is essential. Like humans, dogs that are complimented for a job well done, rather than condemned for a few mistakes along the way, will progress faster and more happily. For example, some dogs instinctively take mouthfuls of food and travel with them a short distance away from the food bowl. Then they drop the food and leave it while they return to the large bowl of food. Suppose you see Duchess doing this. Scold her with the word *bad,* and immediately take her over to the food that fell on the floor. Encourage her to eat the dropped food and praise her as she wipes the floor clean with her tongue. Go to the next deposit of food, and continue the process until the floor is free of dog food. Continue praising your dog throughout the process, and allow her to return to the main bowl. The next night monitor her eating and require that she clean up the dog food she drops before returning to her bowl. If you've had this problem for some time, a week of monitoring might be needed. In this example, you told your dog that a certain behavior was bad, and you praised her when she corrected it. In correcting her eating habits, you guided her into being such a good dog that it would've made her mother cry with pride!

There are several good ways of praising and encouraging your dog for correct behavior. Small pieces of meat or cheese make an excellent incentive. A good chew toy at the end of a training session is another. An intermixing of play and work is fun for both. My favorite two rewards are a good scratch and using the word *good*. Dogs not only love to be scratched, but each one has a favorite place to be scratched. Note the back paw tap-dance when you find that certain spot! The word *good* is a super reward. Use it constantly. In gen-eral, know what pleases your dog, and try to vary the rewards. Praise and encourage her often.

Throughout the book, I will be suggesting the use of food treats for all new training. I support the use of food as a motivator for all initial training because nothing works better. Using food rewards make new lessons quicker to learn and more fun for the dog. However, once the new behavior is learned, phase out the food and substitute other rewards like petting and the word *good*. It is important that your dog listen to you whether you have food or not. Use food treats for new training and only intermittently with previously learned lessons.

Punishment *per se* should never be used. This term implies rough treatment. Never hit your dog. You

Remember, a temptation can easily turn into a behavior problem.

want your dog to love you, not to fear you. If you are presently hitting your dog as a punishment, stop and try using a squirt of water from a squirt bottle instead. The squirt bottle will enable you to correct your dog quickly and from a distance. Rather than punish your dog, try to discipline her. A disciplined dog is one that has developed self-control and obedience. Disciplining your dog will be treated in more detail later on. The basic principle is not to let your dog get away with anything you consider undesirable. The discipline should be gauged to the severity of the crime. In all cases, Duchess should understand that she did something wrong and that she was bad. If a large mess is involved, a long *sit-stay* is in order, so that she can watch while you

clean up the mess. As your dog watches you, tell her she's been bad. Restricting her to a certain area is sometimes an effective method of disciplining her when you are angry or upset. Some area that is away from the family but still within your view is best. The dog must be left there and corrected if she starts to leave the spot. It's your responsibility to release her from the area, not her choice. In removing the dog from the family area, there is a delay in turning the negative into a positive. In this case it might be necessary to give a quick training session in order to put your dog in good standing. You'll find your dog very glad to be back in your good graces.

Most people do not discipline their dogs when friends are visiting.

Thus when the Smiths come over, Duchess runs wild and knows that company means recess! She has been taught that anything goes in front of guests. As long as you make humane corrections, your friends won't mind. Friends and strangers will understand your corrections and appreciate them. You and your dog will gain their respect. There is a chance they'll even be looking forward to their next visit to your home.

Rule 8: Praise or Correct Immediately

The quicker you are to praise or correct, the better off you will be. When Duchess does something that deserves a reaction on your part, give her the proper feedback instantly. Young children who have had a good time drawing with crayons on the kitchen wall will make the connection between their punishment and the crime, even when they are caught and punished hours later. But dogs are different. It's not very effective to discipline a dog for something unless you catch her in the act and discipline her immediately, so that she associates the discipline with the misconduct. Praise works the same way. It must be immediate, so that Duchess can associate the praise with the good thing that she does. Late praise can be misinterpreted by the dog for some misdeed or just happily accepted without understanding. In canine feedback, the quicker the praise or discipline is applied, the better the dog will learn.

Rule 9: Ask Only the Possible

If you ask Duchess to fetch the mailman, you are allowing your dog to fail because the mailman is too heavy and, most likely, he's very unwilling. Likewise, if your dog won't hold anything in her mouth, you shouldn't ask her to retrieve. Stress the positive, and allow your dog only to succeed. The complicated tricks you see canine stars do on TV are accomplished through a gradual training process. The dogs are taught a number of things, each progressing in difficulty, until they master the final trick. If, for some reason, you slip and ask your dog to do something beyond her ability, either allow her to do a portion of what you have asked or physically aid her in succeeding. A shower of praise should then follow. With experience you'll avoid the commands that get you into trouble.

Rule 10: Give a Command Only Once

Why should Duchess react quickly to your command if she

knows you'll repeat it again and again! She won't. Your dog soon learns that she doesn't have to react until your second, third, or fourth command. In Chapter 10 you will be introduced to the word *hurry*. This word will get your dog to obey the original command faster and provide you with an alternative to repeating it. *Hurry* tells Duchess that you know she has heard you the first time and that she should get moving. You'll see your dog perform the command that was given to her seconds earlier without your having to repeat the original command.

Rule 11: Release Each Command

When you command Duchess into a position such as *down* or *sit,*

make her stay in that position until you release her. If you don't, your dog should theoretically stay there for life. The dog whose owner doesn't follow this rule will shortly break from that position when her master's back is turned. The dog knows from experience that she won't be corrected. In this case, the master is reinforcing the dog's disobedience.

Another example is when you're heading out on the town, and Duchess wants to come with you so badly that she's pushing people out of the way to get to the front door. You call her away from the door, tell her to *stay*, and then leave without her. Not seeing you, she decides to move, and is never corrected for breaking a *stay*. Again, you are at fault.

When you give a positioning command, you are committed to enforcing the command and later releasing your dog. Get her used to this. Don't allow her to make the decision. In Chapter 10, I will introduce you to the release word *okay* and how to use it.

Rule 12: Allow Your Dog to Be Good

Leaving Duchess alone in the house with an overflowing trash can might be asking for trouble—especially if you have the remnants of last night's chicken dinner in it. If Duchess has a good time with the trash once, she might just make it a weekly adventure. This negligence on your part applies to many things that make you upset with your dog. A sandwich left on the coffee table when you leave to answer the phone might not be there when you return. Your dog has received a sufficient and tasty reward and is likely to try it again in the future.

Remove all temptations that might cause Duchess to be bad. If she likes chewing on a special throw rug, remove it while you are out of the room. When you are in the room together, replace it and be ready to correct her if she nears it. Place china or other breakable items out of the reach of your dog's tail. When you leave food near the edge of your kitchen counter top, you are tempting your dog needlessly.

The only time you want to present temptations to Duchess is when you are there to make the correction. Let's take the earlier example of your leaving your dog in the same room with the sandwich on the coffee table. The next time you are in approximately the same circumstance, leave the room and wait quietly. Duchess will probably get up and check out what you were eating. She might be coming only to sniff it, but when she does, race into the room and scold her for her attempt to eat your sandwich. If she hasn't budged toward the delicacy she has been smelling, praise her when you enter the room. You might even offer her a small piece of it as a reward.

Rule 13: Train Before Dinner

Practice makes perfect. Unfortunately, time is always in short supply. This rule requires that you run Duchess through a series of commands before you release her to eat dinner. It can be a fifteen-second or a five-minute drill. But be consistent, and make sure you do it before each meal. When dinner is a reward, you'll find that your dog will listen and try hard.

Review the commands that should be familiar to your dog. Do not cover new material at this time. New material can be introduced when you have some spare time. These short sessions will strengthen existing skills. You will both progress quickly, and your dog will enjoy working for her meals. Even with dinner as a final reward, make sure that you verbally reward your dog for doing well. Additional training can be given after your dog has had a chance to eat a bit. This second session, ending in her final release to go eat, is also effective.

Rule 14: Play After Other Training Sessions

With the exception of dinner training, all training sessions should end with play. Put Duchess on *stay* and find her favorite toy or, if possible, have her find it. Your playing with her will be a great reward for her efforts, and it will also give her something to look forward to during every training session. The excitement will show. Experiment with the toys you use. The favorite in my house is a sock for pulling.

Rule 15: Record Your Dog's Progress

Though the Twenty Magic Words are simple, it is still necessary to record your progress on paper. Your dog's progress requires you to be organized. It is the only way consistency and progress can be achieved. If there are other people in your household, this list should be posted, and everyone should be informed of additions and their meaning. Having your dog's language written down on paper will allow you to examine it periodically to note her strengths and weaknesses. With this information you'll be able to overcome her weaknesses and note where additional words might be added.

Many people believe that having an obedient dog is a luxury beyond their reach. They don't realize that they can train their dog to obey them. I am often asked by people if I can train their dog, or they tell me that they've always wanted to send their dog off to obedience school. For a dog to listen to its owner, the owner must participate in the dog's training. Behind every obedient dog is an owner who cares and loves his or her dog. Be very conscious of the rules and your violations of them. Soon you'll condition yourself, and the rules will be a way of life for you. You'll be proud and happy that you understand your dog and that he understands you.

Chapter 5
Your Dog's First Word

As a starting point for all communication with Fifi, it is essential that she recognize her name. It is the first and most important word in her vocabulary. People have names, places have names, and objects have names.

Dogs initially learn their names quickly and with ease. If you are getting a dog, I caution you to carefully select a name you like. Often owners will select lengthy names that later need to be shortened to a nickname. Imagine turning to your dog and commanding, "Sir Edward Dungsburg of Lake Burrough, come!" Both you and your dog will be old before he understands and follows the command.

The purpose of this chapter is to teach you how you can reinforce Fifi's reaction to her name. You must remember that any dog living with people hears thousands of words in the course of a day. Unless you take special care she can't possibly filter out just those that pertain to her. You can help by using her name first whenever you speak to her. It is especially important to use her name first to get her attention before giving her a command.

A drill to practice or just to evaluate Fifi's attention to her name can be done easily. While Fifi is sitting or lying down, begin to walk around the room. Start by holding a food reward, preferably small pieces. Fifi, knowing that you have food, will be all eyes. Continue the circling until her attention fades. When it does, call her name. As soon as her attention focuses on you, throw her a treat. Repeat this several times. If Fifi reacts quickly to her name or watches constantly, you've passed with flying colors! You might want to try the drill again just after you've fed Fifi. This will eliminate food as her main incentive for watching you and will allow her to react mainly to her name. If your dog lacks the desire to watch you or responds slowly at hearing her name, practice this drill daily for a while.

Although using your dog's name to begin a command seems easy and logical, many break this rule. Some dog owners forget to use their dog's name when they give a command. Others give the command first, followed by the dog's name. In the example, "Come on,

Use of your dog's name should immediately draw its attention.

times used in conjunction with another name as in "Come on, Fifi-girl!" These all are nice descriptive nicknames, but the name needed to get your dog's attention immediately is her own! I suggest you avoid variants and use pet names on your deserving spouse or friend to make your dog's life easier.

Fifi," the owner will get Fifi's attention after the command is given, not giving the dog a fair chance to follow the command.

An additional, but avoidable, complication stems from the fact that many owners will also refer to their dog as Baby, Honey, Sugar, Sweetie, Puppy, or Cutie. Boy and Girl are other variants that are sometimes used alone and some-

As you can see, using your dog's name as the start of all communication is important. You'll be getting her attention and then communicating your wishes to her in a logical sequence. The feedback words in Chapter 6 and some of the special commands in Chapter 10 will be your only exceptions.

Chapter 6
Feedback Words – *Good, Bad,* and *No*

In Chapter 4, Rules 7 and 8, the importance of feedback as a means of communicating to your dog what is preferred and what is unacceptable was discussed. Your dog will quickly learn what these feedback words mean. The words in this chapter, along with the words *hurry* and *okay*, found in Chapter 10, are your most useful tools of guidance. These words needn't follow your dog's name. They can be used separately, because they receive the full and immediate attention of your dog.

The Word *Good*

An owner who is happy with his or her dog may use a variety of words: "That's my girl!" "Okay!" "All right!" "You're a fine animal!" Generally the meaning gets communicated to Skipper through the owner's body position and tone of voice. You must restrict your praise to the word *good.* Being consistent in your words of praise will ensure that Skipper will understand that what he did was good. Leave nothing to chance! You want Skipper to understand how happy he has made you in being a good dog. Remember, encourage in Skipper only the behavior that you want. Give him the feedback quickly, and say the word *good* in an excited tone.

The Words *Bad* and *No*

Bad and *no* are the only negative words you need to use. Both words are needed to correct negative behavior: the first for an act already committed, the second for one about to be committed or in progress. There will be times when, like the rest of us, you will want to hurl curse words or milder invectives at your dog. If you do, you will be defeating your purpose. Try your best to limit yourself to *bad* and *no.* When used correctly and consistently, they are the words that will best communicate your views.

Use the word *bad* when Skipper has committed a serious violation and needs to be given a very stern reprimand. If he growls at your neighbor's child, use his collar to control him and make him sit. Then yell at him, using the word *bad.* Often your dog will need to be disciplined for making a mess. Here a time factor is involved while you are cleaning up the mess. Skipper should sit and watch you work. As you clean up, tell him how bad he's been. Occasionally, if your dog lacks the motivation necessary in a training session, it is helpful to call him *bad.* The shock of it can often get your dog to try a little harder. When he does, praise the heck out of him, and he will maintain his enthusiasm. In general the word *bad* will set back your dog's ears, put his tail down, and his face will take on a sad and ashamed expression.

The word *no* will evoke a very different reaction from Skipper. In this case, he will fear a corrector and act very submissively. Use this word when you want to give a quick warning about some temptation that could lead him to being bad. If your dog ignores the warning, a subsequent correction is required. If he is sniffing some freshly baked cookies near the edge of the kitchen counter, a strong "No!" is in order. When he turns away from the sniffing, praise him for listening to you. If your dog runs toward a busy street, you can easily thwart him with the command, "No! Skipper, come."

Here his direction toward the traffic is quickly stopped, and he is called back to safety. The word *no* can also be used in conjunction with other words to communicate to your dog what action should not occur. This can be an advanced warning or a means of scolding in an explanatory way. Later the phrases *no bark, no eat*, *no sniff,* or *no beg* might be incorporated into your dog's language. I have found their application and the application of other combinations extremely valuable.

In summing up, the word *bad* is used when it's too late to yell "No!" Don't worry about which word you use. Both are very negative responses to your dog's unacceptable behavior, and the message will be understood. Use the one that fits the situation or use them both. What's important is that you be consistent in using only these two words, giving the feedback as quickly as possible, and coordinating your tone of voice to match the word's message.

Chapter 7
Major Directives – *Stay, Go,* and *Come*

The directives *stay, go,* and *come* request no movement, a movement away from the speaker, or a movement toward the speaker. They are key words that are used by themselves or in combination with other words. I call them major directives because these three words will enable you to direct Rover anywhere. The need for lateral movement in your dog is not that important, because the *go* command is completely directional with the aid of a hand signal. You merely call Rover to you and send him where you wish. The list of uses of these words is long and practical. Each word and its uses will be discussed in this chapter. Rover's understanding of each word will depend on his ability, your ability to follow the rules in Chapter 4, and how well you follow the training methods described for each word. *Stay, go,* and *come* are the three most important commands to teach your dog and are among the easiest for him to learn.

The Word *Stay*

The *stay* command is given when you want Rover to remain in the place or position you've specified. It could be on the front porch or in a *sit* position while you make his dinner. The *stay* command is a must. It's the basic command in disciplining your dog. You can't discipline him if he's bounding around the room enjoying himself! In training your dog, the *stay* command is necessary for his control and attention. A dog that can do a good *stay* can be taken anywhere, because he can be controlled. If Rover likes to gnaw on small helpless mongrels, a *stay* will keep him from making chew toys out of the poor little things. If the shoe is on the other paw and you own that small helpless dog, a *stay* will allow you to protect it. If Rover is retrieving a ball on the other side of the street and is about to return with it just as a car is approaching, the *stay* could save his neck, tail, hair, and then

It will be discussed in Chapter 10. After a short period of practicing the command, return to your dog and release him. Initially it's a good idea to train Rover that you always return to him before you release him. This will help him to learn faster.

After a week of practicing the *stay* command, Rover should understand it easily. It is now time for you to make a pro of him. Practice the *stay* command in different situations that might cause him to break the command. Be sure that you correct him quickly and reinforce the *stay* in his mind. Below are a few variations you might try in practicing the *stay* command:

1. Give the command when your dog is sitting, lying down, or standing.
2. Increase the time of the *stay.*
3. Drop a book or clang some pot lids to distract your dog.
4. Go outside and try increasing your distance from your dog.
5. Try public places, but remember to think of your dog's safety in the event it breaks.
6. Leave the room, but watch secretly.
7. Add distractions by having neighbors and their dogs walk in front of Rover.

some! Teaching your dog the *stay* command will help his behavior and keep him safe.

Start the training with Rover in a comfortable position and on leash to aid your control. Use the dog's name first, followed by the word *stay.* Walk away from him, but keep a close eye on him. If he breaks forward, quickly push him backward to the original position. Repeat the command, "Rover, stay!" and try again. The *stay* command should not be repeated if Rover is staying adequately (see Chapter 4, Rule 10). Use the word *good,* but expect Rover to break the *stay* command initially, and be there for the correction. He will learn quickly that the *good is* given to praise him and that it's not a release command. The release command is the word *okay.*

Once you've achieved the standard of excellence you have set for the *stay* command, be consistent and don't allow Rover to deviate from it. He will occasionally test you to find out if you'll make a correction. He should understand that once put on *stay,* any crawling is

Left: Tundra in a stay position. Right: She begins to break the stay.

Left: Tundra starts to walk off. Right: She is pushed backward toward the original spot.

Left: Tundra being helped into the sit position. Right: The stay command is repeated.

wrong. This inching, if not corrected immediately, will be considered progress by him, and he will think that it's okay.

The only exception I make for my dogs on *stay* is while they wait for me. Let's say that I'm visiting a friend's house who doesn't own a dog. Out of courtesy to him and his home's lack of dog hair, I *down* my dogs on his front porch and tell them to stay. In this case, I allow them to readjust and make themselves comfortable. They will move to the soft welcome mat or maybe to the corner of the porch to get a better view. As long as they stay on the porch, they understand they are fine, and I won't make a correction. Dogs view things by territories and are easily taught, without a barricade, to stay within certain boundaries. It could be a doorway, an open garage, the base of a tree, or even a sidewalk. As long as you practice the *stay* command occasionally, your dog will continue to take the command seriously.

The Word *Go*

The *go* command is given whenever you desire Rover to move away from you. The uses are practical and helpful. You can direct him to a person, place, or thing. Whenever you need to deliver virtually anything to someone—a message, a can of soda pop, the newspaper, or even a dirty shirt—allow your dog to do it. If Rover is in danger of being made into home plate because your softball team decides they want to drink at your house, direct him under the table or upstairs until the danger subsides.

Sending Rover with the *go* command to retrieve an article can save you much effort, and it's cheaper than hiring a butler! It might be a piece of paper in the yard, your slippers in the closet, or even his own brush for grooming. The *go* command can also be used as a warning when Rover gets in the way. If you're carrying the groceries in and Rover is lying in your path, tell him to *go* and then praise him for obliging. You might even let him help you carry in the groceries. On your next trip from the car, hand him the box of crackers. He'll enjoy helping you.

The word *go* is sometimes used for correction. When Rover is at the dinner table begging for some scraps or maybe a plate of his own, tell him, *"No!"* and tell him, *"Go!"* Teaching your dog the *go* command will allow you to direct him anywhere for whatever reason you desire.

Start training for the word *go* by having your dog sit and dropping a piece of food 5 feet (1.5 m) in front of him. Position yourself next to him in the heel position and say, "Rover, *go!*" as you direct him with your left hand. Run with him up to the meat, and praise him for finding and eating it. Your *go* hand signal should resemble the one pictured above. Be careful to direct him accurately. As Rover learns that it's easy food, increase the distance of the reward,

and hold your position unless he needs some help. Soon you should be able to hide the food behind obstacles, and your friend will find it quickly. This method can be used to direct Rover to a person by having the person hold the reward and, upon Rover's arrival, present it to him.

You can increase your control when using the go command by adding a hand signal.

The Word *Come*

The last of the major directives is the word *come*. Upon hearing this

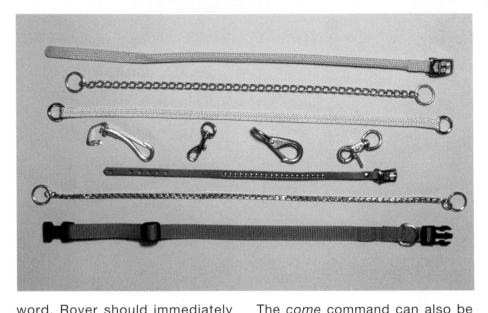

word, Rover should immediately come toward you. Once he arrives, he should sit in front of you and give you his full attention. This command is useful whenever you want to call him to do anything, or even when you might just be lonely.

The *come* command can also be used in conjunction with other commands. In the example, "Rover, come get it!" the *come* is used to guide Rover toward you so that he can find what you want him to get. Whenever the action you want him to perform is between you and him, use the *come* command. Learn by watching his reaction. If the object is too far away on either side of the *come* path back to you, you have three choices. Move in a more direct line with Rover's assignment, use a hand signal to direct him to the proper side, or call him to you and redirect him to the desired spot using the command *go*. The word *come* is by far the most important command for him to know. Only a small percentage of the dog population executes it dependably. With a little correct training, your dog will respond quickly every time.

Left: Put your dog on a stay; attach a rope to the training collar.
Right: Move 10 feet (3 m) away.

Left: Call your dog and pull gently on the rope.
Right: Pull in the slack as the dog approaches.

Left: Back up in a straight line.
Right: Guide your dog into a straight sit.

To prepare training for the word *come*, get a clothesline-sized rope approximately 25 feet (7.6 m) and attach a snap or dog harness clip to one end. Both can be purchased at any hardware store. A special training collar is also very helpful. This collar is sometimes referred to as a choke chain, because it acts as a slip knot would. When one of the two end loops is pulled, the collar tightens around the dog's neck. The name associated with these collars infers strangling and suffocation. Though they can be misused and though some collars on the market do inflict discomfort, most are not cruel if used properly. I find the name "choke chain" upsetting. I ask all dog owners to refer to them as training collars instead. A training collar will give you that extra amount of control needed for corrections. To purchase one, measure the distance around your dog's neck and shop for a collar that is approximately 2 inches (5 cm) longer. The training collar has resulted in some accidental deaths, when dogs jumped over a fence or bush and got their collars caught in the process. If you suspect that Rover could be in danger with such a collar, then remove it after each training session.

Start the training by making Rover sit and telling him to *stay.* Then attach the rope to his collar by using the snap. Go 10 feet (3 m) from him and stand facing him. Hold the rope in both hands and have it almost taut. Have a piece of food ready to reward him. Correct him for any violations of the *stay.* Try a short pause to get his attention and to prepare him to react to your wishes. Call your dog by using his name and the word *come.* If he doesn't move toward you instantly, gently pull on the rope to get him moving and praise him. As the dog is coming toward you, pull up the slack in the rope and back up in a straight line. Taking up the slack will allow you to control his *sit* upon arrival. Backing is used initially for motivating your dog to catch up to you as if he were chasing you in play. Guide him into a *sit* position in front of you and hand him the reward. Be sure to praise him throughout this whole process. Try this several times, and then play with him as a reward. In your next session, review your dog's accomplishments and increase the distance of the *come.* When your dog has the command down pat, remove the rope and try it. If he fails to come immediately when called, run up to him and snap on the lead. Work with the rope a few more times and then try it again without it. Remember patience and praise are your best tools.

Whenever you find your dog responding slowly to the *come* command, a quick practice session will reinforce it in his mind. I keep doggie cookies around the house in different areas to reward my dogs occasionally. If you want to call your dog and have a food reward available, use it. I assure you, Rover

The First Seven Magic Words

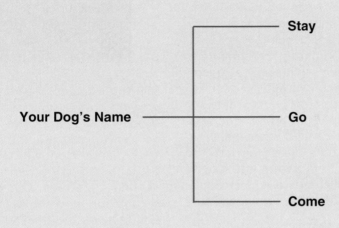

Your Dog's Name

Stay

Go

Come

Good

Bad

No

will come faster the next time. Spoil your dog. He deserves it!

If you have a large house or yard where your dog might be out of yelling range, a bell or whistle can help. Decide on the signal: try your own whistling skills, or buy a whistle or a bell. I give a distinctive two-part whistle in a special tone. Since my orthodontist painfully straightened my incisors, my whistle is always handy. The police recommend a metal whistle on your key chain to scare off or draw attention to an assailant. If your dog is waiting in your car and hears that whistle, you can be sure that the assailant will leave the scene quickly if he sees a dog charging. To teach your dog to respond to a whistle or a bell, go back to the rope training but replace the vocal command with the whistle or bell. Follow the same steps as before. With a little work, your dog will come to you when you use either.

The three major directives—*stay, go,* and *come*—will enable you to direct your dog anywhere with ease and leave him there, if that is your wish. Your dog will be happy because he finally understands you, spends more time with you, gets recognition when he pleases you, and relishes the training sessions because of the special treats you use as rewards. Your dog is now in your control. You now have the means to ensure his safety when you show him off in public.

Chapter 8
Body Positions –
Sit and *Down*

In the previous chapters you learned how to get your dog's attention, how to communicate approval or disapproval, and how to direct or leave your dog anywhere. This chapter concerns itself with Tinker's body positions.

The three major positions a dog assumes are sitting, lying down, and standing. In this chapter I will introduce only the *sit* and the *down* commands and their respective training. In order to keep Tinker's language simple and practical, the *stand* command will not be covered at this time. Chapter 13 will cover it and many other useful words that can be added after you have laid the foundation.

The *sit* and the *down* commands are often used by owners in a confusing manner. Often they are given by using more words than are necessary and using the same words in different commands. Some examples of these are: "Sit up!" "Sit down!" "Lay down!" and "Lie down!" I remind you of this poor communication and ask that you be

very careful to correct any bad habits you've formed.

The *sit* is a position dogs use to enable them to rest their haunches while supporting themselves with their front legs. This command can be used for discipline, instruction, safety, courtesy, and to gain your dog's attention. Once the *sit* command is given, the dog should remain in the *sit* position forever, theoretically, until he is released by you. The release word *okay* will be introduced in Chapter 10. Notice that even though you haven't used the word *stay*, the dog shouldn't budge, just as if you had used it. For this reason, when a longer *sit* is necessary, use the command "Tinker, sit. Stay!" Using the *stay* command will reinforce the idea that he shouldn't budge. The *sit*, though a semiresting position, can be a very boring command for a dog left in that position too long, and a bored dog is tired, unhappy, and unacceptable. Keep your dog excited about training. The dog put on a long *sit* will start to shift its front

Left: Give your dog the sit command. Right: Gently guide your your dog into the sit position.

Left: Control both ends of the dog. Right: Give the stay command.

paws as they tire. This could lead to the dog's breaking the *stay*. Once again, it's your fault. If not corrected for this, the dog may develop the bad habit of shifting its weight, even while doing short *sits*. When practicing a long *sit–stay*, use your head and watch Tinker's expression to gauge the length of the *stay*. A three-minute *stay* is usually plenty for a dog.

The *down* is a position in which Tinker's body is on the floor with his rear legs under him and his front legs extended. The *down* command is useful in long *stays*, because the dog is more comfortable. The uses and training associated with the *sit* also apply to the *down* command. Like the *sit*, once the *down* command is given, the dog should remain in the *down* until released. Add the word *stay* when longer periods are desired. When you call Tinker and *down* him at your feet, be careful that you release him before he breaks the applied *stay*.

Train your dog for the *sit* and the *down* commands at the same time. This is convenient, since with both commands you have to release your dog so that you can repeat them. Find an area for training that is free from distractions, and grab some treats for your dog. Call Tinker and give him a small reward for coming. Your dog already uses the positions. All you have to do is teach him to assume the *sit* or the *down* position when you give the command.

Give your dog the down *command.*

Guide the dog...

...into the down *position.*

Give the stay *command.*

Take time
out for play
after a good
training
session.

Start by saying, "Tinker, sit!" If your dog doesn't move immediately to a *sit* position, guide him gently but quickly into one. Then reward and praise him. The training collar can be used to help you guide him; pull up on the collar while pushing down on his less attractive end. The *stay* command should be added initially to reinforce the fact that your dog should remain in that position. Now try the command, "Tinker, *down!*" If necessary, guide him quickly into the *down* position. Then reward and praise him. Continue alternating the commands. You should find that Tinker will progress rapidly. Don't allow the training to get boring. Move on to other training, or have a play session with your dog. The next day you will find that your dog will be ready to impress you again.

Continue the exercise daily until Tinker responds quickly to each command. As he quickens his response, be more conscious of his position. Some dogs will sit sloppily on the side of their hip or even put a paw out to the side. Determine the standard that you want, and be consistent in correcting Tinker for any

The First Nine
Magic Words

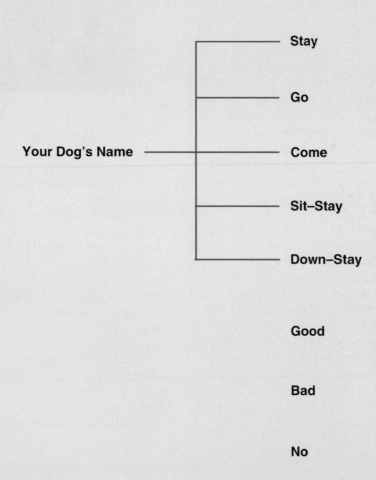

Your Dog's Name ——————— Stay

Go

Come

Sit–Stay

Down–Stay

Good

Bad

No

violations immediately. Approach him and physically adjust his position to what you want. Do not reward or praise him until he has achieved the position you demand of him each time. Occasionally Tinker will have a temporary "lapse of memory," and will do nothing upon hearing a command. He is merely testing you. You should move quickly to make a correction. Do not repeat commands! If Tinker becomes accustomed to your repeating a command, he will soon wait until you have repeated it the second or third time before responding. Make corrections for any forward movement by pushing your dog back to the original spot.

Now that Tinker has mastered the *sit and* the *down* commands, increase your distance from him and practice. No matter how good your dog is, you'll find that there is a certain distance beyond which you'll lose control. Find the greatest distance where you still have control, and slowly increase your range over many sessions. Remember, always allow your dog to succeed! You will progress with him much more quickly.

You now have taught your dog his name and eight basic commands. *Good, bad,* and *no* taught the dog right from wrong. *Stay, go,* and *come* directed him to remain where he is, leave you, or come to you. *Sit* and *down* enabled your dog to assume a certain position. You also learned that you could use combinations of commands, such as *sit-stay* and *down-stay,* to get your dog to remain in a position until released.

If your dog has mastered these commands, you are now ready to teach the secondary commands. If the dog has mastered them sufficiently, I strongly recommend that you keep reviewing them before you proceed.

Chapter 9

Secondary Commands— *Hold, Get, Drop, Bring, Up,* and *Nose*

Secondary commands are used in combination with the major directives *go* and *come* and the body position words *sit* and *down*. These commands can also be used separately when preceded by your dog's name. By teaching Brandy these secondary commands, you will enlarge your range of control over her. You will be able to ask her for the specific action you desire. Because of the special training you will give her, she will be able to respond effortlessly.

When a secondary command is used correctly in conjunction with a major directive, the sentence conveys the message to your dog without any confusion. An example of this is, "Brandy, go, get it." Here the dog's attention is obtained on the first word. The second word starts Brandy moving away from you, and the third word directs her to look for the article and grab it.

The idea that a dog can understand a string of commands in a sentence is a radical one in dog training. Most dog people say that it's impossible. Some claim that their dogs understand sentences, and they very well may. Dogs try to please. If they can pick up the key words in their master's sentence, or maybe a helpful hand signal, they will easily obey the command.

As you and Brandy advance in this language, you'll understand why the logical sentence actually avoids the confusion and stress put on her previously. There will be no limits on the communication you can have with her. Two short sentences will enable Brandy to go to another room, find a specific article, return, and drop it at a previously mentioned spot.

A secondary command can be linked to a body position, as in the example, "Brandy, sit and hold it." Here you first obtain Brandy's attention. The word *sit* gets her to assume the position, and the *hold* commands her to grab the article

Early training for the hold requires gentle pressure under the lower jaw.

article. The *go* and *come* are not used, because Brandy is already in the correct area for the *drop.* Likewise, a specific body position isn't necessary to drop the article in a particular spot. Your goal is to command the desired action in a logical sequence, using a minimum of words to accomplish your purpose. Requesting a *sit* might help Brandy to aim more carefully when dropping your empty pop can in the trash. A missed *drop* could leave drops of pop on the kitchen floor, not to mention your being sentenced to Brandy's doghouse by your otherwise amiable housekeeper!

The words "it" and "and," though not counted in the Twenty Magic Words, are used frequently. I recommend these additives because they complete a command in a logical sentence structure without adding any confusion. Call it a small compromise for humans. The sentences can be delivered gracefully, and your dog will still show ease in following your orders. The additive "and" serves to separate two-word commands for Brandy, and makes it easier for her to understand the sentence command. The additive "it" completes the sentence. Since the word "it" is not accentuated, it will not confuse her.

you hand her. The key words s*it* and *hold* should be emphasized as the command is given. As soon as Brandy understands the s*it* and the *hold* commands separately, combining them in one sentence is quicker for you and easier for her. The command can be used whenever you want her help carrying anything. Even if you can manage a load, get her involved, and she'll be happy from her nose down to her wagging tail.

The secondary commands are also used when no major movement or specific body position is required. In the example, "Brandy, drop it," you are getting her attention and then commanding her to release the

The Word *Hold*

The first four of the six secondary commands are the words *hold, get, drop,* and *bring.* Each of these words represents a specific action involved in basic retrieves. The *hold* command will be learned first because in the *get*, *drop,* and *bring* commands it is essential that Brandy accept an article and hold it in her mouth. She will learn this word when you use it in the following sentence commands:

1. Brandy, *hold* it.
2. Brandy, *come*, *hold* it.
3. Brandy, *sit* and *hold* it.
4. Brandy, *down* and *hold* it.

In the first sentence Brandy is already close enough for you to hand her the article. When the *come* is inserted, you are requesting that Brandy make a debut and accept the item you wish her to *hold.* The sentences "Brandy, sit and hold it" and "Brandy, down and hold it" are useful in handing her an article and in reinforcing the command in Brandy's mind. A specific body position is helpful for her control and attention. Brandy should wait patiently until you give her a further command. This can be useful when there is an unexpected delay. For example, let's say your doorbell rings when Brandy is helping you carry something. Go to the door with her and say, "Brandy, sit and hold it." A stranger at the door gives your dog a very tempting reason to drop the item, break the *stay,* and sniff the stranger. Watch in case you need to make a correction. Regardless of whether a correction is made, when the stranger

leaves, remove the item from Brandy's mouth and praise her, play with her, and thoroughly enjoy her. If the time is short, tell her that she's good.

To teach Brandy to hold an object, first find an object she enjoys holding. I'd suggest her favorite toy, since she undoubtedly has held it many times and has fond memories associated with it. Procure some tasty treats to reward her and call her to you. Ask her to sit, give the command, "Brandy, hold it," and place the article gently in her mouth. Remove the article immediately and reward her. If Brandy is extremely hesitant about holding her toy, try rubbing

Do not press the upper and lower jaws when teaching the hold.

When you need help, your dog will gladly lend a paw—or mouth— as the case may be.

Tundra now takes even the most unusual hold requests in stride.

some of the reward on it. If she won't open her jaws, trick her with a piece of food. Begin to give her a piece of food, but when she opens her mouth, quickly place the article in it. Pull the article out, and then reward her with the food. If your dog accepts the article but seems a bit startled, it's a good sign. You'd be startled too if your friend asked you to hold something in your mouth! Try offering the article again, and make sure that your dog is rewarded quickly each time. You must use your judgment on how hard and long you work in the first training session. If your dog accepts the object easily, continue. But remember that it's your obligation to keep the entire training session on a positive note. Be patient. Continue the training at your dog's pace for a few weeks if necessary.

The next step is to offer Brandy the article, position your free hand underneath her jaw to support it, and release your grip on the article. Do not press her upper and lower jaws together. This is uncomfortable for her and unnecessary. As soon as you are in the correct position, use your free hand to remove the article from her mouth and reward her. Repeat this many times until there is no need for your hand under her jaw. Brandy may test you to see if you will let her get by if she drops the article. If she makes the attempt, make the correction. If she starts to spit it out, put your hand under her jaw and repeat the command, "Brandy, hold it." If you are slow and the article falls to the floor, quickly place the article back in her mouth and command her to *hold* it.

Even though the remaining three sentences containing the *hold* command are easy, each should be practiced separately. The first command is, "Brandy, come hold it." Place her on a *stay,* and walk 10 feet (3 m) away from her. Turn to her, hold out the article, and give her the command. Help her all you can at the beginning, and remember to reward her when you remove the article from her mouth. The next two sentences, "Brandy, sit and hold it" and "Brandy, down and hold it," are also easy. Put your dog in a standing position, say the commands, and hand her the article. If she doesn't assume the proper body position, help her into it, and offer her the article to hold. I say help because a severe correction will lessen her desire to learn the new material. Keep the duration of the *hold* short at first, and reward her. You should also train your dog to be able to hold an item while going from a *sit* to a *down* position and vice versa. In this case repeating the *hold* part of the command reinforces the command and prevents any mistakes. Your dog should continue to hold the article until you take it from her, until you give her the command to *drop* it, or until your dog's great recall comes from heaven!

The training process for *hold is* easy because of the gradual steps. You've allowed Brandy to succeed in each step, and in the process the learning has been clear and quick. Continue by increasing the time an object is held and by using different objects. You'll find that Brandy hesitates to accept some articles because of their weight, size, shape, or composition. You'll also find that in the process of training she has picked up the hand signal for *hold.* Every time you told her to "hold it," she saw your hand coming toward her with an article for her to grab. You've conditioned her not only to your verbal command but to your hand signal, thus making the communication of the command easier for her to understand and obey.

The Word *Get*

You are now ready to teach the command *get*. In your dog's new language, the *get* command will be restricted to the act of acquiring the article. Some trainers insist that *get* means the whole process of obtaining the article, holding it, bringing it, and either holding it or dropping it on arrival. In this case, *get* simply communicates the specific action desired.

The word *get* will increase your dog's vocabulary if you use it in the following sentences:

1. Brandy, *get* it.
2. Brandy, *go, get* it.
3. Brandy, *come, get* it.
4. Brandy, *go up* and *get* it.

Use the first of these when the article is within your dog's reach, and she doesn't need to move toward the article. In the second sentence, "Brandy, go get it," the go is inserted to send Brandy away from you and toward the article you've chosen for her to grab. When the come is inserted in the third sentence, you are requesting Brandy to travel toward you, find the article, and grab it. The last sentence, using the word up, will be discussed later in this chapter.

Dogs vary greatly in learning the word get. Many dogs instinctively chase an article that is thrown, and most of them will grab it. For the dog that does, teaching the get will involve only some additional con-

trol. The dog that presently isn't a good retriever has the instinct. It simply hasn't been developed. This fact makes it easy to teach your pet. Almost all dogs get daily practice in the get command in one way or another. They grab and carry toys around, and if a piece of food is thrown their way, they do a beautiful get! While the time it takes to teach different dogs the get command will vary, every dog is capable of learning it in a very short time, and all of them will enjoy carrying out the command over and over.

The procedure for teaching Brandy to get an object will use her favorite toy again and some tasty treats. It is essential that you get her in a playing mood. It will be more effective if you get down on the floor with her. Using her toy, play with her, and build up her interest in the toy. Drop the toy in front of her, and say in an enthusiastic voice, "Brandy, get it." Often tapping the floor next to the toy or wiggling the toy will help. If she succeeds in grabbing it, quickly take it away from her and reward her. If your dog fails to grab it, go back to playing and try again. Use your own judgment as to when you should stop the lesson. Let your patience and your dog's enthusiasm be your guide.

If Brandy doesn't seem to be catching on at all, the only answer is to get sneaky. Rub some of the tasty treat on the toy, play with it, and drop it again. This time when you drop it, leave a treat on top of it and give the command. Point out the treat if necessary. When Brandy reaches to grab it, place the toy, food and all, in Brandy's mouth. Quickly remove the toy while praising her, and allow her to chew the treat. Condition her by doing this over and over. Then repeat the steps, but omit the treat. This time Brandy will move toward the toy to look for the food. When she gets close, help move the toy into her mouth. Praise her as you exchange the toy for a treat. Practice these initial steps until a high percentage of success is achieved. Soon your dog will grab the toy quickly and receive her reward.

As you continue Brandy's training, throw the toy away from her while saying, "Brandy, go, get it." Her reactions will determine if additional steps are needed. It's essential that she run to the toy. If she does not, try the throw and the command again. This time run out with her. Put a leash on her for control if necessary. Then stop her at the right spot and reward her. If Brandy runs to the toy and then bounds off, put her on *stay*, and place the toy and a piece of food 10 feet (3 m) in front of her. Go back to Brandy and give her the command. This time when she stops for the food, be there with her, and keep her from continuing on by using the leash. Once your dog understands that she has to travel immediately to the toy, use the techniques you've used earlier to help her pick it up.

When your dog gets the toy with ease, try the command, "Brandy, come, get it." Place your dog on *stay*, and walk away from her. Turn toward her, place her toy 4 feet (1.2 m) in front of you, and give the command. In this exercise it is important that your dog never be allowed to pass by the article she is asked to get. If she does, stop her immediately, push her back, and reinforce the *get* command. As you practice, move the toy closer to your dog, but continue to keep it in a direct line between the two of you. You will find that your dog adapts easily to this command because she understands the *come* and the *get* from her previous training.

The Word *Drop*

The next secondary command for your dog to learn is the *drop.* This refers to your dog's action of releasing an article she is holding. Using the major directives *stay, go,* and *come,* enables you to position your dog anywhere. Once your dog is positioned, the article can be dropped in a specific spot. The word *drop* will increase Brandy's vocabulary if you use it in the following sentences:

1. Brandy, *drop* it.
2. Brandy, *go, drop* it.
3. Brandy, *come, drop* it.
4. Brandy, *go up* and *drop* it.

The sentence "Brandy, drop it," can be used either when Brandy happens to be in a convenient spot for the article to be released or when the dropping is of major importance compared to the spot. If a particular spot is required, the major directives will be implemented. When the *drop* is used in conjunction with *go* and *come,* Brandy will delay the *drop* and travel in the specified direction looking for the proper *drop* zone and then drop it. I refer to it as a *drop* zone because there will be certain places that your dog will understand are for dropping things. An empty box, the kitchen trash can, the toy box, the coffee table, and the clothes basket are just some of the places she'll quickly recognize. The more you practice,

Practicing the command, "Go, drop it.*"*

To advance your dog further on the *get,* try different articles and different locations in placing the articles. When you send your dog to get an article, make sure that you avoid any confusion as to which article you're asking her to grab. Also, keep in mind that the *get* applies to her grabbing the article and not necessarily to her returning the article to you. Later the word *bring* will be utilized to get her to bring the article to you.

the more versatility you'll have in your *drop*. The last sentence, using the word *drop* and also the word *up*, will be discussed later in this chapter.

To teach your dog the word *drop,* find an article that would be uncomfortable for her to hold. The idea is to make your dog want to drop it badly enough so that dropping it will actually be a reward for her. This article should not be the one you used in training your dog for the *hold* command. Pick an object that she has a hard time holding. Since your dog will be dropping it, make sure your selection can't be damaged and that you're on a carpeted floor. You might try a screwdriver, a tablespoon, a hair roller, an egg whisk, or even a set of metal measuring spoons.

With the proper article and some treats in hand, put Brandy in a *sit* and have her hold the article. Yell in an excited tone, "Brandy, drop it!" At the same time, offer her a treat and gently knock the article out of her mouth, praising her as you do so. Repeat this exercise until Brandy starts dropping the article on her own in order to eat the food you're offering. If you still have trouble, wait a longer period on the *drop,* switch the article to make it less pleasing to hold, or offer her something she can't refuse for the treat. Your dog should catch on quickly.

When using the *drop* command, it is unwise to catch the article as your dog drops it. If you reach out to catch it, Brandy will soon begin to hold it until you reach out for it. It will become a hand signal for her to drop the article. This will be undesirable when you want her to drop something far away from you with a verbal command only. You won't be there to give her a hand signal. Also, if you send your dog to deliver the article to someone, you'll want her to hold it until the article is taken from her mouth.

The procedure for teaching the command, "Brandy, go, drop it," is an easy one. Ideally, it is best to have a large empty room that is free from all distractions and also a large receptacle to catch the article dropped. Realistically, an empty box in an empty corner will do. The corner will direct her attention to the box you've placed in it and also control her path of travel between you and the corner. To make a *drop* easy for your dog, the box needs to be about four inches (10 cm) lower than your dog's mouth when she is standing. If necessary, cut off the top few inches of the box. Use an article that is uncomfortable to hold. Have your dog *sit* about one foot (30 cm) in front of the box and *hold* the article. Give the command, "Brandy, go, drop it." If Brandy doesn't move, ease her into a standing position while you support the article beneath her jaw. Allow the article to drop when her mouth is over the box. Reward your dog with a treat and a lot of praise. Repeat this until you're ready to increase the distance before the *drop,* change the

her *hold* the article. Place the box in front of her and position yourself in front of both of them. Say the command and, if necessary, help her to drop the article into the box. By this time the *drop* and *come* are understood, and this exercise will be merely for practice.

The Word *Bring*

The secondary command *bring* directs Brandy to return immediately to the speaker while carrying the article she's holding or the one she's just picked up. Adding this word to the language is necessary because it represents a specific action not covered by the word *hold.* The command *bring is* a delivery to the person speaking. In Chapter 13 I will discuss the use of the word *take.* This word will allow Brandy to make a delivery of an article to another person. *Bring is* always used in a sentence having the following form: "Brandy, come, bring it." Since your dog's action is always toward you, the major directive word *come* helps her understand you. You'll find that since the command is very descriptive, your dog will easily learn it and perform it consistently.

Practicing the command, "Come, drop it."

To teach your dog the *bring* command, put her in a *sit* position and have her *hold* her toy. Walk ten feet away from her, turn, and face her. Then give the command, "Brandy, come, bring it." Praise her first attempt as she starts moving toward you. If she drops the article,

placement of the box, or use a different type of *drop* zone.

The teaching of the sentence "Brandy, come, drop it," is quite similar. Use the same article and box, but this time leave Brandy in the corner in a *sit-stay,* and have run up to her, put the article in her mouth, and reinforce the *hold* command. Then quickly back up and repeat, "Brandy, come, bring it." As your dog comes up to you with the article in her mouth, give support to her jaw to keep her from dropping the article, and gently guide her into a *sit* position. Remove the article, and replace it with a treat. Repeat this many times until your dog is proficient in performing the command.

Use your inventiveness to further your dog's mastery of the word *bring.* If you have a helper, sit on opposite sides of a room and take turns giving the command to Brandy. Each time, after you reward her, just ask her to *hold* it, and wait for the helper to call her. It is very important that you always require that your dog assume a *sit* position and that she hold the article until you take it. This results in a very attractive delivery.

Once you've succeeded in teaching Brandy the first four of the secondary commands, give her the following test. This will indicate where Brandy needs some more practice. Place an article 20 feet (6 m) away, give these commands in sequence, and make the necessary corrections.

1. Brandy, *go, get* it.
2. Brandy, *sit* and *hold* it.
3. Brandy, *drop* it.
4. Brandy, *get* it.
5. Brandy, *down* and *hold* it.
6. Brandy, *come, bring* it.

The Word *Up*

The fifth secondary command for Brandy to learn is the word *up*. The word *up* will be used for positioning her above the floor, the ground, or a particular level. You will be able to direct her *up* on couches and beds, into truck cabs, up stairs, etc. Please note that the *up* command does not refer to the action of jumping but to your dog's positioning herself above the level she's on. In Chapter 13 you will have the option of using the command *jump* for the purpose of directing Brandy to jump over anything specified. The word *up* will increase her vocabulary when you use it in the following sentences:

1. Brandy, *go, up.*
2. Brandy, *go up,* and *get* it.
3. Brandy, *go up*, and *drop* it.
4. Brandy, *come, up.*

Brandy will catch on quickly to the word *up*, because it will usually mean a reward for her. Getting up on the couch with you is a privilege, and very comfortable too! Dogs will be eager for the opportunity to climb into the family car. Some will like the comfort, some the view, and others will appreciate not being left behind. For training, it will be helpful if you allow Brandy *up* on at least one chair in the house. In our family we have designated a "dog chair" on which the dogs are allowed to stay whenever they wish. They love their privilege and respect the other furniture in the house. If you are a new dog owner and haven't started a furniture policy yet, I suggest that your dogs shouldn't be allowed up on anything without your direct command.

Start the training for the word *up* by having Brandy sit facing a chair approximately 2 feet (.6 m) away. Have your treats ready, and stand behind the chair so that the chair is between you and your dog. Give the command, "Brandy, come, up," while patting the cushion of the chair. When she jumps up, quickly help her into a comfortable position and reward her. This should be easy for most dogs. Initially they will respond more to the hand signal of patting the cushion. If Brandy has difficulty, it's probably because of your previous training with regard to the furniture. Try to entice her with food. Help her up into the chair, if necessary, while showering praise on her. Be patient, and keep everything positive and happy. She'll catch on.

As soon as she is responding to "Brandy, come, up," start increasing her distance away from the chair before you give the command. Then proceed by not patting the chair any more. Now back up a few feet in a line with Brandy and the chair, and try it again. Continue the practice, backing up each time. Remember to reward her each time she succeeds. Take it step by step. If she gets confused, repeat the previous steps. You might want to use different chairs. Or try sitting on a couch when you give the com-

mand. In the future when you call your dog upstairs, give the command, "Brandy, come, up." You'll find it even will help Brandy to locate you.

Now that your dog has learned "Brandy, come, up," it is time to teach her the "Brandy, go, up" command. Position her and yourself a few feet in front of a chair. Give the command, take a step forward, pat the chair, and reward her when she gets up on the chair. Increase the distance slowly and continue, traveling quickly to the chair with her each time. Decrease the patting of the chair each time until the patting of the chair is unnecessary. Next, instead of traveling to the chair, allow your hand to swing out toward the chair as you give the command. If your dog is slow to respond, quickly run toward the chair, directing her. Soon she'll get it!

As soon as your dog understands the word *up,* experiment with the sentences, "Brandy, go up, and drop it," and "Brandy, go up, and get it." Both should be easy for your dog because she understands the components of the command. Merely help her through it a few times, making the necessary corrections. Remember to keep things very positive by using frequent praise.

Have your dog sit at your side, hand her a favorite article, and say, "Brandy, hold it." Use the same chair and the same spot as in the *up* training. Give the command,

"Brandy, go up, and drop it." Initially put a lot of emphasis on the "Brandy, go up" portion of the command. If your dog drops the article on the way up, quickly put it back in her mouth, pause, and tell her to *hold* it. If your dog succeeds in jumping up while holding on to the article but fails to drop it, remain silent. The reason for the silence is to tell her that her mission is not finished yet. During this silence, dogs will either drop the article, as you requested, or hold it, awaiting your instructions. If necessary, repeat the "drop it," praise her thoroughly, and repeat the exercise. If your dog is having problems, stop the exercise and go back to practicing the elements of the *hold* and *up* commands. It's important that she doesn't get a negative feeling for the command. Go slowly enough to allow her to succeed.

To teach your dog the command, "Brandy, go up, and get it," start a playing session with her favorite toy. Once she is in an excited state, quickly put her in a *sit-stay,* and throw the toy to the rear of the seat of the practice chair. Give the command, but make sure she doesn't grab the article without jumping up onto the chair first. A strong "No!" will work if she reaches for it. This should be followed by repeating the "Brandy, go up" command. As soon as she jumps up, direct her to get it. You probably won't need to give the command, "Brandy, come, bring it."

Your dog will quickly return to the playing session with her toy. Play a bit and try it again.

The four sentences that I've introduced you to are the most practical. You will be able to use the word *up* in combination with other words you have taught thus far. I haven't mentioned them, because it's usually more successful to direct Brandy up with one command and then follow it with any other command you might desire. You will notice that *up* is always used with the major directives *go* or *come.* The reason for this is that the word *up* always implies a necessary movement to a particular level.

Use the up *command to direct your dog to a higher level, such as up the stairs.*

The First Fifteen
Magic Words

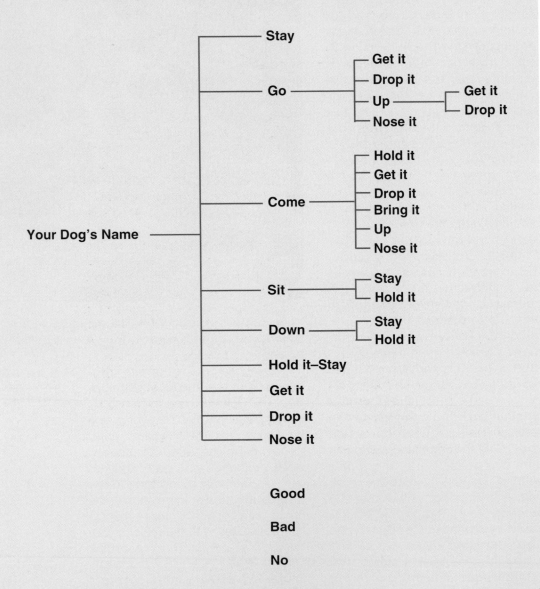

Your Dog's Name

- Stay
- Go
  - Get it
  - Drop it
  - Up
    - Get it
    - Drop it
  - Nose it
- Come
  - Hold it
  - Get it
  - Drop it
  - Bring it
  - Up
  - Nose it
- Sit
  - Stay
  - Hold it
- Down
  - Stay
  - Hold it
- Hold it–Stay
- Get it
- Drop it
- Nose it

Good

Bad

No

The Word *Nose*

The last of the secondary commands is the word *nose.* The training for this word is found in Chapter 3. If Brandy is not presently nosing a bell to communicate her needs, then review Chapter 3. Don't proceed with the following exercises until Brandy has mastered nosing the bells. Once understood, the *nose* command can be used for other purposes. You can have fun directing her to open or close doors or drawers and to retrieve large balls or similar objects that she can't grab.

The word *nose* will be added to Brandy's vocabulary when you use it in the following sentences:

1. Brandy, *nose* it.
2. Brandy, *go, nose* it.
3. Brandy, *come, nose* it.

Select the proper sentence based on the movement required of your dog. To avoid confusion, don't conduct advanced *nose* training near the bells. You may use treats as rewards in this advanced work, but remember to be patient and take it step by step. Use the same methods that you used on the bell, and your progress will be assured.

The secondary commands you've learned in this chapter will widen your range of control over your dog. Allowing Brandy to be helpful will increase her happiness and even save you steps. You should require that she pick up after herself. Have her place her toys in her toy box when they're not in use. If you see an item on the floor or couch that needs to be thrown away, direct her to do it for you. If you need the morning paper, your slippers, or even her brush, your dog can easily be trained to accommodate you. If you sleep with your door closed at night, allow her to close it for you. Permit her to help you daily, and reward her for it. It's a sure way to increase your mutual love and happiness.

Chapter 10

Special Commands— *Look, Bark, Walk, Okay,* and *Hurry*

All of the special command words are important, practical, and serve to make the life of you and your dog easier and more enjoyable. Several are absolutely necessary for the effective use of your dog's new language.

The Word *Look*

The first of these command words is *look*. In teaching it and in using it, always precede it with your dog's name. Saying your dog's name gets your dog to look at you. When you say, "Lady, look," your purpose is to keep her looking at you until you release her or command her to do something else. The *look* command is also beneficial in introducing new material.

The training for *look* is very similar to the training you gave Lady for responding to her name. Start with a food reward, and put her on a *stay*. Walk around the room, grab something from a shelf, and give the command, "Lady, look." Praise your dog continually while she is looking at you, so that she continues to do so. Make the object look more interesting by turning or moving it. After a few seconds of her full attention, throw a food reward her way and tell her she is a good dog. You can lengthen her attention span with practice. You might try using different objects to keep her interest fresh. If Lady turns away from you and will not watch you, make it easier for her to watch you. Position her in a dark room, and have her look at you through a partially open door. Sit on the floor in front of the door in a lighted room and try again, using different articles to get her attention. If you are still having trouble, use a more tempting food reward and more interesting objects, such as a new squeaky toy or a steak bone. You shouldn't have much of a problem teaching the word *look* to her. Remember to lengthen her attention span slowly, allowing her to

After you've taught your dog the twenty magic words, he will be well behaved wherever you go.

succeed each time. The clap hand signal can also be used with this command. You will be introduced to it in Chapter 12.

The Word *Bark*

The seventeenth word in the language is the word *bark*. Though you might think it difficult to teach the *bark* command to Lady, I assure you it's not. Almost every dog barks naturally. All that's needed is to train her to do it on command. I recommend this word to all dog owners for the added security the command provides as well as for enhancing their dog's personality. In your home a dog's bark is usually enough to make a potential intruder try somewhere else. Even if the dog sounds small, the intruder won't want to mess with an alarm device equipped with teeth. If you are out late at night walking your dog and see some not-so-neighborly-looking characters approaching, it's useful to whisper the *bark* command to your dog and have her begin barking. I would then cross the street, keeping an eye on the strangers, or walk to a well-lit house with my barking dog. If the individuals you are passing in the night are law-abiding citizens, they will appreciate your avoiding them!

Lady's personality can be enhanced when she learns to bark on command. Though a bark is a sharp, loud vocal expression, it can be a beautiful sound to you. This is especially true if Lady barks only when she hears noises or upon your request. The encouragement of your dog's vocal abilities will lead to other sounds. Howls, little woofs, moans, or whimpers can easily be obtained from your dog by rewarding her each time she gives you the sound. A talking dog has more character!

You can add the word *bark* to Lady's vocabulary by using it in the following sentences:

1. Lady, *bark.*
2. Lady, *go, bark.*
3. Lady, *come, bark.*

The first sentence, "Lady, bark," is used when an immediate vocal response is desired. The major directives *go* and *come* are combined with the *bark* when movement is needed. These two sentences can be used in the home for protection. If you and Lady are watching television, and you hear a noise in the kitchen, send her to check it out, using the command, "Lady, go, bark." Soon she will understand which noises she should be concerned with. If she is asleep in another room, and you hear a strange sound, call her with, "Lady, come, bark." If there is possible danger, you'll want her on the job.

To teach Lady to bark on command, it is necessary that you use a stimulant that makes her bark. Try to duplicate situations in which your dog will bark naturally, then praise her for it. If possible, stop her barking by gently holding her muzzle. Then release it, and give her the *bark* command. Reward her with a treat and repeat the exercise. Often, if you make a barking sound or Lady hears another dog bark, she will bark also. Dogs often bark out of fear of the unknown.

With the help of a friend or another member of the family, a variety of situations can be set up. First, it is best to trick Lady into thinking that only you and she are in the house. Have everybody else leave for a period of time. Your helper can either sneak into a back room or stay outside the house. Ask your helper to make strange noises by pounding on the side of the house, scratching at the door, or playing a recorded tape of strange voices. Your helper should make noises until Lady barks. When she stops, the helper should wait for about twenty seconds before repeating the noise. This will reward Lady for her barking, since she will think that her barking stopped the intruder. Whenever you are in the house with Lady and hear a sound, adopt a worried expression and tell her to bark. Run to the area of the noise as you praise her for barking. When she has barked for a short period, hand her a treat. This will reward her further and keep her from overreacting to a small noise. A good guard dog will bark a bit and then stop to listen for additional noises. A Halloween mask viewed through a window may provoke Lady to bark. When she barks, the person wearing the mask should pretend to be scared and leave.

In these setup situations it is best not to let Lady know that the stranger is a friend of hers. This can be accomplished easily by asking that your helper delay entering the house for five minutes. Specify in advance that your helper repeat the noise cycle a certain number of times and then quit. This way both of you will know when the training has ended. Wait with Lady and listen in silence. Afterward, play with her as a final reward. Work daily on the *bark* command until you can whisper it and get an appropriate and immediate response. (Depending upon the circumstances, it might sometimes be wise to inform your neighbors of your training plans. Otherwise, they might call the police to investigate your intruder.)

The Word *Walk*

The word *walk* pertains to Lady's daily constitutional for exercise and the excretion of waste. Even if you have a backyard to let her use for this purpose, the need for walking her may arise when you are at Aunt Martha's house, playing in a city park, or on a summer vacation. The word *walk* will need little work before your dog understands it. The real training will be in controlling the walk. Public pressure requires you to walk your dog in suitable places. A dog that can walk in a designated area can be taken anywhere with confidence.

Let's say that you have an errand to run in town. Always ask yourself the following questions before taking Lady with you:

1. Is the errand a long one or a quick stop?
2. If you have to leave her in the car, will it be too hot for her, or will she be in danger of being stolen?
3. If you can't leave her in the car, is there an area just inside or outside the building where you can *down* her and watch her?
4. If you plan to enter the building with your dog, does the building have tenants or a guard who might object?
5. Do you have everything you need with you—a leash, water, and maybe some rewards?
6. Will your trip take so long that it will be necessary to walk her?
7. Will there be a suitable place to walk her?

If your answer to question six is yes, then you need to answer question seven with a yes. If you think you might have trouble finding a suitable place to give her a walk at your destination, stop at an appropriate spot before you get there. Never take her for a walk in someone else's yard, in front of an office building, or anywhere where there are many people. Pick areas such as an empty field or the edge of a parking lot that is full of weeds. These areas are less likely to offend anyone.

If you get stuck and need to walk your dog in a park, pick an area by a trash can. You can often grab a couple pieces of trash to use as a scoop for cleanup. Another suggestion is to carry a box of sandwich baggies in your car for such occasions. Turn the baggie inside out, put your hand inside it and grab your dog's deposit. Then just turn the baggie right side out. It'll keep the "freshness" in, and that can be an advantage.

The word *walk* can be used in the following sentences:

1. Lady, *walk?*
2. Lady, go, *walk.*
3. Lady, come, *walk.*

The first sentence is a question that you may ask your dog. Different dogs will react differently. By their reaction to your question, you'll be able to gauge how immediate their need is. Some will look at you sadly or begin crying, others will get excited and start jumping around. If Lady is at home, she can use the bell to tell you. But when she is out with you, the question comes in handy. Remember to change the tone of your voice on the word *walk* to signify a question.

The sentence, "Lady, go, walk," is used both for permission and direction. You're telling her that it is all right to relieve herself in the area you're directing her to. Approach the area, stop on the perimeter facing the center of the walk area, and give the command.

The sentence, "Lady, come, walk," can be used in two ways. The first is when your position is between Lady and the walk area.

Here you give your dog permission to pass you and walk. The second way is when she has traveled toward the outside perimeter of a walk area and is ready to relieve herself in somebody's yard. In this case giving the command will move Lady's sniffing toward you and into the proper area.

The word *walk is* an important word to your dog. The training involves controlling the when and the where of the *walk.* It requires daily practice until sufficient control is reached, then occasional review to maintain it. Even if you have a large backyard, and it's convenient and easy to let Lady out in the mornings, don't. Get dressed, then head out the front door with Lady on her leash. Mornings are perfect for the initial practice because it's a sure thing that Lady needs a walk. You can delay the walk until she

One of Tundra's favorite spots: plenty of room to run and lots of privacy.

The Walk should also be practiced on a leash. Here we take advantage of a weedy area at the edge of a parking lot.

noses the bell and really gets close to the realization of her needs.

Find a suitable spot for the walk. A restricted area is best at first. If possible, pick one that has two clear borders (a fence and a sidewalk). Your full attention should be given to Lady, so avoid distractions and practice control. Snap off the leash, and give Lady permission by saying, "Lady, go, walk." If she approaches the border of the desired area, give a strong "No!" then give the command, "Lady, come, walk." Initially she might test you and not listen. If she doesn't obey, run to her, stop her in her quest for relief, and snap the leash back on. Return to your original position on the border, and make Lady sit at your side for a few seconds. Then release her by saying again, "Lady, go, walk." Although this may seem like a lengthy procedure, it is necessary to teach her that she must listen to you—especially if she wants that walk. Praise her for using the proper area.

Daily practice for two weeks will give Lady the control she needs. If possible, try a different area each day. Some should be large areas with no borders; others should be very small areas of gravel, weeds, or grass. The large borderless areas are the hard ones. Here you must make imaginary borders and stick to them. If you don't, your dog can travel far and get out of your range of control, chase another dog, or sniff a scared passerby. Take Lady for a walk in the afternoon and evening when she nudges the bell. This will give you a chance to show her that the *walk* must be controlled then, too.

The *walk* should also be practiced on a leash. This may be awkward for you and unnatural for your dog. But after a while, both of you will get accustomed to it. Local laws may require that you use a leash, but even where they don't, it can be a good practice. The training in giving the *walk* command on a leash will be valuable if you have to walk your dog in a place where there are a lot of people or traffic and her safety is endangered.

Although your dog's need to relieve herself is simply a need of Nature, it can be embarrassing. If you attain good control of your dog and are careful to select the best *walk* spots you can, it will be less embarrassing. Speed up the whole process so you attract as little attention as possible. The twentieth "magic" word, *hurry,* will be a big help to you in doing this.

The Word *Okay*

The last two words in Lady's twenty-word vocabulary are the words *okay* and *hurry.* These words share common ground in that they are two-syllable words. In Chapter 1, I mentioned the importance of confining Lady's vocabulary to one-syllable words. Using only one-syllable words simplifies the language and avoids much confusion. The words *okay* and *hurry* are allowed as exceptions because they are always used by themselves. These words are not to be used together or in combination with other words that would result in confusion for your dog. *Okay* and *hurry* are also the best and the most natural words to use for the purpose that they fulfill.

The word *okay* is used as a release command. It gives Lady the approval to break a *stay* or, if you're involved in a training session, it dismisses her to play, sleep, chase birds, or whatever she wishes to do. In using *okay,* your tone of voice will be important. It should sound both happy and excited.

Care should be taken not to use *good* as a release word or *okay* for praise. Keep their meanings—and their uses—separate. Always correct Lady if she breaks a *stay* on the word *good. Good* implies doing the proper thing; it is not permission to play. Refer to Chapter 6 for a review of the word *good.* If *okay* is accidentally used as a praise word, it can put Lady's safety in jeopardy. Let us say that you're on a busy street corner and for some reason you've forgotten your leash. Using the word *okay* at this time instead of *good* could lead to a disastrous break in her control. Never use *okay* or, for that matter, anything other than a quiet *good* when you're in a situation that might be dangerous.

A release word or signal is an important part of Lady's vocabulary. Without it she will eventually disobey you and release herself, and you can't blame her. It is impossible to give Lady the option of releasing herself and still maintain control over her. You'll find the word *okay* easy to use and effective in properly releasing your dog from a *stay* or a training session. Remember that an implied *stay* also needs a release. If you have downed Lady next to you, don't allow her to move until you release her. She will quickly understand that *okay* means that she is on her own. Just be consistent in its use.

The Word *Hurry*

The twentieth magic word is *hurry.* This word demands an immediate response. The command is given in an enthusiastic tone conveying eagerness and urgency. Rule 10 in Chapter 4 says that you should give a command only once. If you repeat a command, you are teaching Lady that she doesn't

The Twenty Magic Words

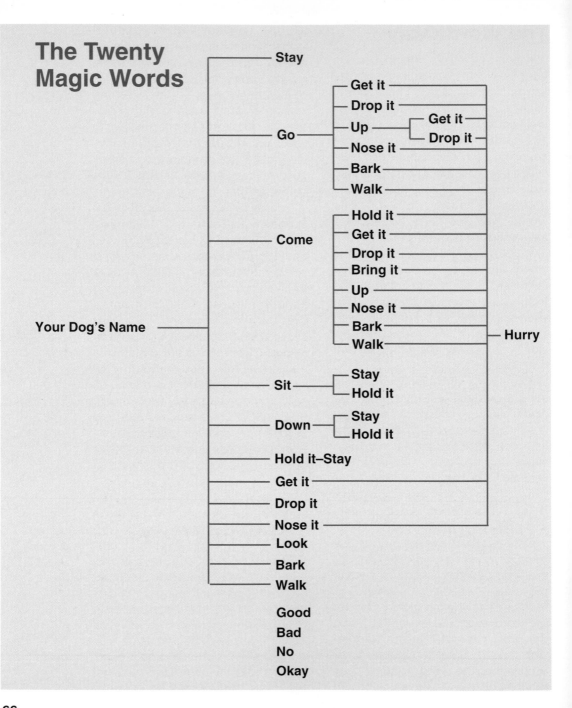

Your Dog's Name

- Stay
- Go
  - Get it
  - Drop it
  - Up
    - Get it
    - Drop it
  - Nose it
  - Bark
  - Walk
- Come
  - Hold it
  - Get it
  - Drop it
  - Bring it
  - Up
  - Nose it
  - Bark
  - Walk
- Sit
  - Stay
  - Hold it
- Down
  - Stay
  - Hold it
- Hold it–Stay
- Get it
- Drop it
- Nose it
- Look
- Bark
- Walk

Hurry

Good
Bad
No
Okay

have to listen to you the first time. The word *hurry is* a safety valve that keeps you from repeating the original command and tells Lady to hasten in obeying it. You'll be amazed when she completes the assigned task after ignoring the command so completely that you'd swear she never heard it.

There is not much training involved in teaching the word *hurry.* It's more a matter of your learning how and when to use it. The word *hurry is* used by itself and doesn't follow your dog's name. Use it when Lady is slow in responding to a command or when she doesn't respond at all. Generally speaking, you can use it after a command containing the major directive *go* or *come* and whenever a *get* or *nose* is used. Other commands are tricky, and you need a feeling for their use. You have two basic alternatives in correcting either a slow response or no response: Make a correction or use the word *hurry.* Use your judgment about making a physical correction, depending on the situation. If you are in a public place or among friends at home, I wouldn't make a correction unless it's a behavior problem involving a stranger or friend. Commands like *sit, down,* and *drop* imply no major movement, so you don't want to wait all day for a simple request. Here a correction or possibly a review of the training involved in the command would be in order.

When Lady has mastered the special commands, she has acquired Twenty Magic Words. *Look, bark,* and *walk* are helpful words in making life easier and more enjoyable for both you and her. Since you will always release her after giving her certain commands, you will be using the word *okay* frequently. *Hurry* is a command that will speed her on her way to carrying out a previous command. The continuous use of the commands and careful observation of the rules in Chapter 6 will allow your dog to maintain her understanding of the language, and help her in expanding her vocabulary.

Chapter 11
A Quiz

The aim of this quiz is to get you to think about future decisions concerning your use of the language. Read the questions carefully. They present situations requiring your decision. The answers are meant to be tricky. Analyze the questions thoroughly, and choose the best answer. I expect you to fall into my traps, so don't be discouraged. The correct answers and an explanation are below the choices.

Question 1: Your dog, Red, is in the living room with your children watching television. You want Red to help carry something for you. You go over and stand in the doorway of the living room with the article in your hand. What should you do?

A. Say, "Come, get it."
B. Say, "Come, get it and hold it."
C. Say, "Red, come, hold it."
D. Ask one of the kids to tell Red to get it.
E. Say, "Hold it."

Always use your dog's name first to get his attention, unless you use a feedback word or a special com-

mand. In this situation, with the presence of children and a television set, it is essential that you get his attention first before telling him what you want him to do. Answer C is the only one that starts properly. Examine it more closely. The word *come* is necessary because there is a distance between the doorway and the television area. Red needs to travel toward you before he can take the article. The *hold* command is necessary because you want Red to take the article on his arrival. For those of you who picked answers A or B, "Come, get it," applies to looking for and picking up an article on the way to you, not after arrival. "Red, come, hold it," is the proper command to use.

Question 2: As you walk out of your bedroom, you catch Red sniffing the kitchen trash. What should you do?

A. Say, "Red, no!"
B. Feed Red immediately, because he must be hungry
C. Say, "Red, go!"
D. Say, "Red, bad!"
E. Say, "No!"

This became a better picture because of the hold command.

Answers A, C, and D are not correct because you've used Red's name. You don't want to call his attention and, upon receiving it, yell at him. This could teach Red not to give you his attention at all. Using his name before a feedback word also keeps the feedback from reaching him sooner. It is important that the feedback be immediate (see Chapter 4, Rule 8). Answer C should be rejected because it doesn't even contain a feedback word. Answer B is wrong since feeding Red immediately will just teach him to sniff the trash whenever he's hungry. The proper command to use is a sharp "No!"

Question 3: Red is up on the couch with you, and you want him to leave. What should you do?

A. Say, "Red, go, walk," and then praise him as he starts walking.
B. Say, "Red, go," and then praise him as he gets to the floor.
C. Say, "Red, walk," and then praise him as he gets to the floor.
D. Ask a family member to call Red.
E. Say, "Red, go," and then praise him as he starts moving.

The command *walk is* contained in answers A and C. I wouldn't advise using either of these answers, because the word *walk* gives him permission to relieve himself. Answer D will work. But if you want Red to leave, don't ask someone else to command him to do so. Answers B and E use the same phraseology, "Red, go." In both, you get Red's attention and tell him to leave. The answers differ as to when you administer the praise. The proper answer is B, because it is better timing to give Red praise as he gets to the floor. He has fulfilled his assignment, leaving you on the couch and putting himself on the floor. When you praise Red for starting to move, the praise could be misinterpreted. Often he will hear the praise and, thinking he did what you desired him to do, will lie down again, glorying in the thought that he has pleased you!

Question 4: You've asked Red if he wants a walk. He goes to the door and misses in his attempt to nudge the communication bell. Now he is waiting at the door, looking at you. What should you do?

A. Command him saying, "Red, get it and drop it."
B. Say, "Red, go, nose it."
C. No command should be given, and a correction should be made.
D. Say, "Red, nose it."
E. Say," Hurry!"

Red heard the question and tried to answer that he needed a walk, but missed the bell. Since you never commanded Red to nudge the bell, answers C and E should be eliminated. You shouldn't make a correction or hurry a command that has not been given. Answer A is asking Red to retrieve and drop the bell—a tough order, when it is enough trouble just to ring it! Answer B includes the word *go*. This is unnecessary and

confusing because Red is standing next to the door. "Red, nose it," is the proper command to use.

Question 5: Red picked up your sock thinking it might make a good toy. What's the best way of handling the situation?

A. Let him have it.
B. Say, "No!"
C. Say, "No!" then say, "Red, drop it," and praise him when he does.
D. Say, "Red, come, bring it," and praise him while he does.
E. Lightly slap Red's nose, tell him he's bad, and remove the sock from his mouth.

Socks do make great pull toys. If you have a clean but holey sock that you can donate to the cause, try it. Answer A is not the one we are looking for, though. If you have his toy sock next to your sock, he can easily tell his by the smell. No offense intended! There is no excuse for him to pick up your sock. Answer D is wrong because it is not good to have Red bring you an object that you don't even want him to grab. Answers B and E all work, since either one will communicate the idea. However, I prefer answer C because it is a very positive way of correcting Red. You've caught Red doing something wrong and told him so. Then you have him drop it and praise him for not holding it. The praise could be taken a step further by grabbing one (or several) of Red's toys and playing with him. This reinforces which are his toys. Whenever possible, you should use a positive way of correcting him.

Question 6: You asked Red to get an article, and he did. But he didn't return with it, and you wanted him to. He's just standing there holding it. What should you do?

A. Say, "Red, come, bring it."
B. Say, "Red, get it and bring it."
C. Sat, "Red, hold it and bring it."
D. Praise him for not bringing it.
E. Take a break until your dog is more interested.

The word *get* required Red only to pick up the particular article you specified. Red should be allowed to return with it if you don't indicate what else he should do with it. Answer D is not correct, since it doesn't solve the problem of his not bringing the article to you. Answers B and C contain the words *get* and *hold.* These are repetitious commands, since Red is presently holding the article. Answer E should be rejected because your dog needs to obey you when you require it, not at his own convenience. In this example, you wanted Red to return with the article. Since you commanded him only to get it, another command is required to get him to completely satisfy your wishes. That command is found in answer A, "Red, come, bring it."

Question 7: Red is arriving with an item you've asked him to bring. On the way to you, he accidentally drops it. What should you do?

A. Pause and wait to see if he grabs it. If he does, praise him; if he doesn't, give the command, "Red, come," and then send him back for it saying, "Red, go, get it."
B. As he starts to drop it, give him the command to *drop* it and praise him.
C. Make a physical correction by running to him and putting the article in his mouth.
D. Order your dog to *sit* and yell at him that he's bad.
E. Pause and wait to see if he grabs it. If he does, praise him; if he doesn't, give the command, "Red, get it," and, if necessary, "Red, come, bring it."

There is no reason to yell at your dog for this. As far as a physical correction goes, none is necessary unless this mistake is becoming a bad habit. Even then, it's probably your fault. You might want to go back and review your training of *hold*. The method in answer B should be avoided because Red should be required to succeed. Answers A and E have the correct idea. Red accidentally dropped the article but might recover it on his own. He can surely learn to do so with a little practice. Be sure to allow him a short pause to recover it. Answer A will produce the results, but does it the long way around. Answer E is the better of the two.

Question 8: You want Red to wake up your son, Billy, by jumping on his bed. What should you do?

A. Whisper, "Red, go, jump up," while directing him with your outstretched arm toward the bed.
B. Stand at the door of the room and whisper the command, "Red, go, get Billy."
C. Pick up Red and toss him on the bed while praising him.
D. Whisper, "Red, go up," while directing him with your outstretched arm toward the bed.
E. Leave Red on a stay, go over to the bed, and whisper the command, "Red, come, jump up."

Answers A and E contain the word "jump." "Jump" is not in Red's language, and thus these answers should be rejected. Answer B sends Red to retrieve Billy. This would wake Billy, but he might be a little heavy for Red to carry. Answer C should be eliminated because Red is more than capable of doing it himself. The proper command to whisper is in answer D, "Red, *go up.*" The outstretched arm will help direct Red to what you want him to jump on.

Question 9: Red helped you carry the groceries from the car, and you asked him to *sit* and *hold* it when you got to the kitchen because your hands were full. You finally are able to take the article from his mouth, and you are ready to dismiss him. What should you do?

A. Tell him he's good and to *go.*
B. Give the command, "Okay!" then praise and reward him.
C. Give the command, "Red, go," then praise and reward him.
D. Give the command, "Scat, varmint!" and throw something at him.
E. Give the command, "Red, go on," then praise and reward him.

If your answer was D, just close this book and go back to training your goldfish! Answers A, C, and E are incorrect because each answer uses the word *go* to release Red. The problem in using the word *go* is that you want to use this command only for directing your dog to a person, place, or thing. If you use it as a release command, you will weaken its value as a directing command. Answer B is correct. It uses the release word *okay* followed by a lot of praise and a tidbit of food as a reward.

Question 10: You've taken Red for a walk*,* and he appears to be quite finished. You've given the *come* command, and he's moving slowly toward you. What should you do?

A. Tell him, "Hurry!"
B. Allow him to have more time.
C. Don't ever take him for a walk again. Let him suffer. That will teach him!
D. Tell him he's bad and repeat the *come* command.
E. Make a firm correction.

Answer C should be the answer you reject immediately. Floating eyeballs are not healthy for a dog! Answer B is unnecessary if you've given Red plenty of time to walk. If you really think you might have called him too soon then, once he arrives, you should send him to walk again. Just use the "Red, go, walk" command. Answers D and E are unacceptable because Red is obeying you, no matter how slowly. There is no reason to yell at your dog or make a physical correction. All you want to do is speed Red up a bit. If one of these were your answer, you might want to go back and review your training of the word *come* with Red. Answer A, "Hurry!" *is* the proper response. You might begin to walk away from the area. If you do, this will reinforce the *hurry* command, and Red will quickly catch up with you.

I hope this quiz has made you realize that situations will often arise in which you are not sure of what to do. There is much more to using the Twenty Magic Words than just knowing them.

When a new situation arises, react the best you can. Afterward review the situation and your reaction to it. If you have made a mistake, try to remember not to make it again when a similar situation arises.

Chapter 12
Hand Signals

Hand signals are gestures done with the hand to convey a command. Often the whole arm and even the body are involved. These signals can be useful in reinforcing an oral command or in performing certain tricks. They can also be used in getting a dog to assume a certain body position at a particular location and then to make minor adjustments in the location or position. If you recall, I have already recommended that hand signals should sometimes be used with the commands *go* and *up*.

Dogs often depend on our body positions as well as our hand signals. These visual signals help them to understand and interpret our commands and even our wishes. We often display our feelings through our facial expressions and our body movements. Dogs know when we are upset, happy, or tired. They can also predict what we are about to do by watching our body movements. They know when we're heading for work or play, or to that most heavenly of all places—where the dog food is

kept! If you usually take a stroll with Duke in the evenings, you trigger his excitement by merely starting for the closet to change shoes.

We will take advantage of our dog's ability to interpret visual signals. This chapter will introduce you to the five hand signals that I have found most helpful and practical. Later you will undoubtedly develop some of your own as you find a need for them.

The Handclap

The first of the five hand signals is the handclap. Unlike the other hand signals, which give a visual signal to your dog, this one signals Duke through his hearing. It is a special hand signal because it is one of the few possible ways to make a loud and distinct noise with your hands. It is also an easy signal to make. It has one shortcoming, however, in that it lacks flexibility. It can make only one type of sound. For this reason, the handclap is used to give one—and only one—

message: getting your dog's immediate attention. Although it conveys only one message, that message is important, and you can use it often.

The handclap is an excellent attention getter. When you are in a situation where the noise level is high, a loud handclap can get your dog's attention without your having to yell a command.

Upon hearing the handclap, Duke should stop what he's doing, look at you, and wait for further instructions. It carries the same meaning for him as the command, "Duke, look." You should give only one crisp clap for the handclap. Do not give a series of claps, as if you were applauding someone.

Once you can get Duke's attention by means of the handclap, you can regain control of him when he makes a mistake in carrying out a command, when he is being bad, when you want him to greet a newly arrived guest, or even when you want him to lavish a slobbery hello on Aunt Martha.

You'll find the handclap particularly helpful when you are showing off your beloved canine's talents to the neighborhood rowdies. Children are a constant distraction to most dogs, as you know. The handclap will help you keep control of your dog in front of them. When entertaining children, I have observed that my dogs often mistake the children's clapping in applause as a hand signal, and the dogs immediately pay attention to me! Instead of being a distraction,

this helps me move the show along.

To train your dog to respond to the handclap, use the same method you used in teaching him to respond to his name. Read a book or a magazine, and wait patiently until his attention is on something else. Then clap. As his eyes turn to look at you, throw him a small piece of food as a reward. Return to your reading until his attention is again on something else. Then clap again to get his attention. Do this over and over, each time increasing the time between his response and your reward. This will gradually increase the time you can hold his attention.

The Directed *Go*

The directed *go* hand signal can be used with any of the commands containing the word *go*. It is a guide to get Duke to travel in the necessary direction to fulfill his task. If there are several items on the floor, the oral command, "Duke, go, get it," supplemented by an appropriate hand signal will help Duke select the proper item. Similarly, when trying to get Duke to drop an article in the proper spot, it is confusing to Duke if you make him guess where he should drop it. The command, "Duke, go, drop it," supplemented by a suitable hand signal will help him to drop the article in the correct drop zone. This hand signal is meant to complement the

communication given in the oral command. Duke will appreciate the direction you give him as he heads out to fulfill his assignment.

To perform the directed *go* hand signal it is necessary to position yourself next to Duke. This way you're both facing the direction of the task, and you're close enough to him to send him accurately to the proper spot. Let's say that the task is to retrieve a piece of crumpled paper on the floor. Use the command, "Duke, go, get it," as you swing out your hand and arm (the one on Duke's side) toward the article. Your knees should be bent, so that you can maintain your balance as you reach out as far as possible with your "guidance system." You should make every effort

As you finish extending your arm, give the command go.

A wall will help your dog stay on course when practicing the directed go *hand signal.*

have confidence in your outstretched arm. For now, though, swing your directing arm and hand a little bit to the inside of where it should be. He will still veer a little, but he'll be heading in the right direction. When giving the next ten or so directed *go* hand signals, slowly readjust your direction so that your signal is accurately pointed. Duke's initial fear of being too close to the swinging hand signal will gradually diminish.

A wall can also be used to keep Duke from veering until he adjusts to the hand signal. Position yourself so that the wall is on the side to which he veers. The wall will keep Duke from veering in that direction and will help to guide him to his correct destination. Regardless of the method you choose, practice will polish the directed *go* hand signal, and you will be able to send Duke in the direction you want.

to give the hand signal at Duke's eye level. Though you should always make your hand signals as clear as possible, sometimes it's necessary to give only an abbreviated directed *go* hand signal. At other times even a good hand signal will be beyond Duke's ability to understand, and you will have to help him further with additional commands and signals.

When you initially use the directed *go* hand signal, some dogs will veer to the side and not go in the proper direction. Since you are giving the hand signal at Duke's eye level, Duke might veer to the outside. With practice he will learn to

The Directed *Come*

The directed *come* hand signal can be used when the *come* command is used with the words *get, drop, up,* or *nose.* These commands require your dog to travel toward you; look for the article, the drop zone, the higher elevation, or the item to be pushed; and then complete the requested command. When the assignment linked to the *come* command is in a direct line between you and Duke, the mission is an easy one. When it is not, you have two choices. One is to shift your position so that the assignment is directly between you and him. The other is to use a hand signal to direct Duke to veer off the path. If you are resting in a nice, soft easy chair while enjoying a movie and a cold drink, moving might require a major effort on your part. Don't waste your energy. The hand signal will communicate the message and add to your dog's versatility. The directed *come* hand signal is meant to complement the oral command and adjust the path of Duke's *come* to suit your needs. In Duke's initial training, avoid using the usual *drop* zones, the usual *up* areas, and the usual items that he *noses.*

Start by leaving Duke on a *stay* and placing an article 10 feet (3 m) in front of him. Position yourself five feet (1.5 m) away from the article, with the article several feet off the direct line between you and Duke. Say your dog's name, give the directed *come* hand signal, and give the rest of the command, "Come, get it." As you continue to practice this, the hand signal can eventually be given at the same time as the vocal command. Duke will learn to watch you for the additional instruction.

The directed *come* hand signal is performed by swinging your arm straight out to the side. Use the arm on the side where Duke is to go— that is, indicate the article on your right with your right arm. Keep the hand signal at Duke's eye level by bending your knees a bit. Have your hand open, with the palm facing him, to allow the arm to receive his full attention. Leave your arm extended to the side until the article is grabbed. When Duke returns with the item, praise him and reward him with a tidbit of food.

Repeat the exercise, alternating the article's position from one side to the other. Each time place the article farther off the direct line between you and Duke. Never allow him to pass by the article you want him to pick up. If he starts to pass it, quickly push him back and tell him to get it. When he does get it, return to your original position and let the praise flow.

Within a short time Duke should be grabbing the article regardless of the side it's on or the distance it's away from the direct line. Now introduce two articles for his selection, and use the exercise you used to teach him to look at things. Put each article several feet off the direct line between the two of you and on opposite sides. If possible, use identical articles. If not, have the article that you've been working with on the side that you will request. Later use two equally unfamiliar items. Practice getting your dog to select the designated article. Don't allow him to grab the wrong one. With a sharp "No!" back him up into the original position and let him try again. This time make sure he sees your hand signal. If necessary, move your whole body toward the same side. If you still have trou-

The directed come hand signal.
Left: Put your dog on a stay.
Right: Swing your arm straight out to the side as you give the command to get it.

Left: The article is retrieved.
Right: The dog delivers the article.

ble communicating the message, return to the single-article exercise and practice some more.

There are limits on how far you can go in developing the directed *come* hand signal. There is a point at which Duke will get confused if an article is too far to the side. Stay within the limits of his ability, and allow him to succeed. If the item desired is extremely far off the direct line, call him to you and send him to it by using the more precise directed *go* hand signal.

If you have children or pets, your floors will usually be strewn with items that are perfect for advanced training purposes. In our house we blame this clutter phenomenon on ghosts, on increased sunspot activity, and on the gravitational pull of the earth—not on ourselves, of course! Once the directed *come* hand signal is learned, Duke can perfect his skills in both the directed *go* and the directed *come* hand signals. Allow your dog to save you all that bending and stooping. Where else can you find a helper who's happy to work for dog cookies?

The *Down*

The *down* hand signal can be useful in many situations where the oral command *down* has weaknesses. Oral commands can interrupt conversations and movie plots if you're watching a late movie. If the noise level is high, your oral

The abbreviated down *hand signal.*

The down
hand signal.
*Left: Swing
your arm back.
Right: Allow it
to continue
to swing up
and over
your head.*

*Left: Continue
the swing in
front of you.
Right: The
end of the
swing.*

command can become lost in the din. At a distance or when you're competing with the wind, the hand signal will be more effective than a weak oral command. Sometimes the hand signal will be easier to use because your mouth is full! The *down* hand signal will give you yet another communication tool. Both you and Duke will find it easy.

The stay *hand signal.*

There are two ways of giving the *down* hand signal. One way has more intense movement; it is intended to be used at a distance. The other way is an abbreviated form of the first; it is used when you are fairly close to Duke. The abbreviated *down* hand signal is done without swinging the arm. Merely put your open hand out in front of you with the palm facing down, and thrust it quickly downward. To give the *down* hand signal that is effective at a distance, stand with your hands at your side and your body facing Duke. Swing your arm away from your dog toward your backside. Allow it to swing up and over your head. Continue the swinging motion, bringing the arm in front of you palm down, and return it to your side. Each time your arm is overhead, accelerate its downward motion in a forceful way. Always try to do this hand signal in front and to the side of your body. At a distance Duke will find it hard to see a hand signal that blends into your body.

To teach Duke to respond to the *down* hand signal, place him on a *sit* while you kneel two feet or so in front of him. Give the abbreviated hand signal as you say, "Down!" Reward him immediately, and then tell him to sit. Your kneeling position gives Duke the best possible view of your hand signal and makes it possible for you to end your hand signal by hitting the floor with your hand. This seems to make the hand signal even clearer. Repeat this exercise five times, and then try it without giving the oral command. If Duke doesn't move, say "Hurry!" and help him quickly but gently to the *down* position; then lavish praise on him. Once he carries out the command consistently, stop hitting the floor with your hand, and continue to practice. The next step in training is to try the exercise on your feet, in different areas of the house, and at increased distances. Once the abbreviated *down* hand

The hand giving the signal is motionless in front of his nose, making the message clear.

To teach Duke the *stay* hand signal, repeat the same steps you used in the *stay* oral command. Have Duke sit, and give him the *stay* hand signal. Walk away and, if he breaks his position, make a correction and repeat the hand signal. Remember to release him properly with the word *okay* and praise him. Practice the *stay* hand signal just as you practiced the oral command. Use as many different situations as possible.

signal is learned, the long-distance *down* hand signal can be taught easily. Start teaching it up close and extend your range gradually.

The *Stay*

The *stay* hand signal is an alternative to the oral *stay* command. Like the *down* hand signal, you will use the *stay* hand signal when you find it more convenient than the oral command. This hand signal is performed with the hand open and the palm facing the dog. The fingers can be pointing to the side, down, or up. This hand signal should be given as close to Duke's nose as possible, but it is still quite functional at short distances. The hand signal should be made deliberately and last for at least a full second.

The hand signals you've learned in this chapter are meant to help you. They are designed to be clear from the dog's point of view. Other hand signals may be added if you find a beneficial use for them. I caution you to allow your hand signals only to aid your language and not to replace it. Oral commands can be turned on and off simply by using your dog's name and then the release word *okay*. Your body signals cannot be turned off.

Chapter 13

Taking the Language a Few Steps Farther

This chapter suggests new words that you may want to add to your dog's vocabulary. New words, however, should not be added until you and Muffin have become proficient in using the first twenty words. The words you've learned make up the essential foundation for you to use in communicating with her. The Twenty Magic Words work because of their simplicity. Keep the new words you choose to introduce simple, and do not introduce them too soon or too fast. To do so may destroy much of the training you have already achieved. Care must be taken not to confuse an already functional and effective language.

From reading this book and working closely with Muffin, you now have a way of communicating with her. When you introduce new material to her, you need to employ all the teaching skills that you have learned and not take any shortcuts.

There are many things for you to consider in choosing words to add to Muffin's vocabulary. I will mention

only the most important ones. The word you choose should be highly useful, one you need and can use frequently. It should contain only one syllable if possible. It should not rhyme with or be similar to words used in the commands you have previously taught. It should also be distinct from previous words in its meaning. The action that you intend to elicit by its use should be distinct from the actions you have been able to obtain with any previous commands. Be sure to consider your choice of new words with care. You will not want them to interfere with or undo any of the previous training you have achieved.

Categories of New Words

First, I will cover some of the general categories of possible new words you may wish to introduce. These categories will include different groups of words that might be useful to you. A basic guide to the training involved will also be included.

Names of Persons

If you teach Muffin the names of the members of your household, you will not only be able to direct her to each one but also to make deliveries to them. Just think how convenient it will be when Dad calls from upstairs for a screwdriver or Mom wants your dirty shirt to wash.

All of these situations are easily handled by using the major directive *go* in combination with the person's name. Just hand Muffin the object or message. Say, "Muffin, *go* to Joey," and send her off in the right direction to find him. The requested delivery should always be followed with a cookie when your dog returns to you. Start Muffin's habit of returning to you by calling her after the delivery is made. That way your dog will receive oral praise at her destination, return to you quickly for a cookie, and be ready for another delivery if necessary.

To teach your dog to differentiate between different people's names, initially train her to travel to the designated person without an item to deliver. Upon arrival, have the person reward her with a cookie and praise her. Sharpen Muffin's knowledge further by having two of the people she knows stand on the other side of the room from you and her. Send Muffin to a specific person, who should praise her

when she arrives. If she goes to the wrong person, repeat the command until Muffin finds the right person. You will find that your dog will pick it up quickly.

Names of Places

Words signifying certain places can also be very useful in Muffin's vocabulary. If you desire to send her away from you, it will be helpful to specify where you wish her to go. The place words that you may wish to teach her without bogging down the language are "wall," "door," "stairs," "bed," and "house." "Wall" is any upright structure that divides or encloses; "door" refers to the doorway of a room; "stairs" are a series of steps between levels; "bed" is the area or the pad where Muffin sleeps at night; and "house" refers to her doghouse, if she has one. These words are not applicable to all dogs. Some dogs won't have houses, and others will have no reason to know what a doorway is. One of our dogs enjoys lying at the door and guarding the entrance.

All these words are used in combination with the major directive *go*. An example would be, "Muffin, *go* to bed." Begin training her by starting close to the place you want her to go. Then give the command, run her over to that place, and reward her. Once Muffin does it on her own, increase the distance between the starting place and where you want her to go. This method should work easily for all places except "stairs." "Stairs" will be discussed later in this chapter.

Compound commands should be delayed until Muffin has mastered the new words suggested in this chapter. A compound command is a sentence such as, "Muffin, go to the wall and drop it," or "Muffin, go to the door and bark." For the time being it is best to limit your command to sending her to a certain place and then giving her a separate command after she gets there.

Names of Objects

You may want to include in Muffin's vocabulary the names of a few objects that you will use frequently. Some of the names that I find useful are the names of my dogs' hairbrush, the newspaper, certain of their toys, and their favorite foods. The hairbrush is simply "brush;" the newspaper is "paper;" the toys have simple but distinctive names such as "chew," "squeaky," "sock," and "ball;" and the several food items have names such as "cookie," "steak," and "meat."

To teach Muffin to get her brush, for instance, I would say, "Muffin, go, get the brush." Then with hand signals I would guide her to the brush, call it again by its name, and help her pick it up. After rewarding her with praise, I would gradually increase the distance between the brush and the place where I give the command. I have found it convenient to keep her brush in an open shoe box on the closet floor. This provides a good drop zone for the brush's return.

Though it's hard for me to brush my dog daily, allowing her to get the brush and put it away helps me to get the occasional grooming done.

Teaching Muffin to get the paper can be done in the same way. You'll see how helpful it is when you can get her to do it for you. It will keep you from getting some vital parts of your anatomy frozen in winter and from being reported by your affable neighbors for indecent exposure on some overly hot morning in summer.

Requesting certain toys can keep the play session interesting. To teach Muffin the names of several of her toys, get her to look at one of her toys while you say the name of the toy. When you have done this for two of the toys, place them a distance apart on the open floor. Then use a command like, "Muffin, go, get the ball" and guide her to the ball. Gradually guide her less and less. Command her to get the other toy, guiding her to it at first. Then alternate your command to get the ball or the other toy. Eventually you can introduce a third toy and maybe a fourth toy.

The name-dropping of a favorite food can be used to increase the excitement for an upcoming training session. After a couple of minutes of anticipation, grab the food item and begin the training. Teaching Muffin the names of her favorite foods is rather easy. She will learn quickly if you say the name of what you are giving her each time you reward her.

In teaching the crawl, tempt your dog to stretch for food.

Use your other hand to keep the dog in the down position.

Then allow your dog to reach the tidbit.

Tricks

You can add words to Muffin's vocabulary that direct her to carry out special tricks. Some examples of these are *paw, shake, bow, crawl,* and *roll.* Try to limit your commands to one word.

To get her to roll over, use the word *roll,* not the phrase "roll over." An exception might be in trying to make her look even smarter. For example, instead of asking Muffin for her paw, ask for a specific paw and teach her the difference between the commands *left paw* and *right paw.* Your friends will think you have the smartest dog in the neighborhood!

Tricks will be limited only by your imagination. When training your dog to do a trick, it is necessary to proceed step by step and to reward her as she succeeds in accomplishing each step. For instance, a crawl is easily achieved by first giving her the command, "Muffin, down." With a piece of food in your hand, tempt her to stretch forward for it. Use your other hand to gently keep her in the *down* position if she attempts to get up. Allow her to succeed in reaching the food, but require her to reach a little farther each time. Tapping the floor with the food works well as a hand signal. The *come* command can help in communicating to Muffin that she should move toward you for the food. In the crawl, she needs to shift her front paws to move forward and scoot her hindquarters along. If necessary, you can help her by moving one paw at a time so

that she gets the idea and also the food reward.

Vocal Sounds

If your dog makes a variety of vocal sounds, words can be added to his or her language to define them. The vocal expressions possible are "little woof," "cry," "moan," "howl," "bark," and "growl." I recommend teaching your dog the word associated with the vocal noise, unless it happens to be "cry" or "growl." I caution you here because a crying dog is very annoying to most people, and a growling dog can sound very dangerous. The bark of a dog is sufficient for the sake of protection.

A talking dog has an enriched personality compared with one that doesn't talk. Strongly encourage

Top Left:
"Beg!"
Top Right:
"Play dead!"
Left: "Pray!"

Muffin whenever she makes a sound that you'd like to hear more often. Make a big fuss over her. Once Muffin is making that particular sound often, associate a word to describe it while you praise her. In your training sessions, ask Muffin to make the sound while tempting her with a piece of food. Often mimicking the particular sound will help. If your dog is trying hard but no sound comes out, you might want to reward her efforts. Have patience. It can take a lot of encouragement for Muffin to make a particular vocal sound.

Although I love talking dogs, I should mention a problem associated with them. A great talker can interrupt conversations and phone calls. In case you have overtaught the vocal sounds, and your little friend has become a constant gabber and interrupts you, the command word *quiet* can be used. Initially, you will have to teach Muffin the meaning of the word by using a squirt bottle of water. Give Muffin the oral command, "Quiet!" If she talks, give her one squirt and reinforce the command *quiet.* Praise her for being quiet and be prepared for another correction. She'll pick up the meaning quickly.

Hungry?—Thirsty?

The last of the general categories of beneficial words are questions. In Chapter 10, the question "Walk?" was used to determine a need of your dog. The questions I'm suggesting will also do the same. The

single word questions are "Hungry?" or "Food?" and "Thirsty?" or "Water?" The alternative word in each case is given so that you may select the ones that you would feel more comfortable using. Whichever you choose, stick to it and be consistent in its use.

Since most dogs are always hungry, the first question can be used to gauge hunger. In this case though, the measurement is not as important as the excitement generated. This excitement can be properly channeled to make for a great training session. I suggest that you prepare Muffin's food so that it's ready to give to her, and then go back to what you were doing. When your dog approaches you, ask her if she is hungry in an excited but questioning voice. As soon as some excitement is reached, proceed with a training session (see Chapter 4, Rule 13). The meaning of the question itself will be learned quickly through its nightly repetition. Muffin will learn to effectively coax you into training her. Once the training session has begun, you'll see a dog do everything in her power to please you.

The single-word question "Thirsty?" or "Water?" is used to judge Muffin's thirst when the communication bell (see Chapter 3) is not available. If you have been traveling for a few hours or she looks hot and is drooling, it's a safe bet that she's thirsty. The question also comes in handy when you're not sure if Muffin can wait a while or if she's uncomfortably thirsty. Here asking the question and observing her reaction will be your key. Her understanding of the question will again be learned from the repetition of the word while she is thirsty.

When Muffin nudges the communication bell meant for water, go over, fill the dish, and ask her the question. If she gets excited, nudges the bell again, or even vocalizes, allow her to drink by placing the filled dish on the floor. When traveling, use the question word "Thirsty?" or "Water?" only if you have a supply of water with you. I always take a jug and water dish along in the car for my dog if I think we might be gone for a while. Whatever you do, never use these question words to tease your dog. I'm sure you don't want her turning you in to the ASPCA!

The last part of this chapter is concerned with ten valuable words that can be added to Muffin's vocabulary. Though these words fit into one of the general categories previously mentioned, their possible existence and importance easily could be overlooked. These words can be very useful and deserve the extra explanation given.

The Word *Back*

The word *back is* used to move Muffin backward. If her placement is a bit too far forward, move her back. This will happen when Muffin crowds you too closely, when she's in danger of being accidentally stepped on by less aware com-

pany, or as a correction when you command her *down* but she takes an extra step toward you. The command *back is* used in conjunction with Muffin's name or by itself, depending on her attention.

To teach Muffin to *back,* find or create a narrow passageway that will prevent her from turning around. This can be done by placing three chairs in a hallway to make it narrower or by pulling a bed close enough to a wall. Just leave enough room for her width, no matter how broad your beam has become.

You'll be teaching Muffin by using a hand signal for *back.* This signal is very similar to the *stay* hand signal in that the palm of your fully opened hand is facing her. In the *back* hand signal, though, the hand pushes back and forth toward her.

A bed next to a wall makes a great passageway for teaching the word back.

First, put Muffin in the passageway, say the oral command, and use the hand signal at her eye level. While giving the hand signal, allow your palm to come up to Muffin's nose and push gently. This should cause Muffin to move backward. Shower praise on her, or even give her a food reward, and then repeat the exercise. As you practice, slowly widen the passageway until Muffin can execute the command in a completely open area such as your living room. If she begins to turn around instead of backing up at your command, return to practicing in a narrow passageway again.

For backing up a long distance I prefer using the hand signal to the oral command, so that I don't have to repeat the oral command several times. Just say the oral command to get Muffin's attention, and follow it by using the hand signal until she has backed far enough. For showing-off purposes, it's more spectacular to have her back up in whatever body position she is in when you ask her to back up. If she is in a *down* position, she should back up in a *down* position. If she is in a *sit* position, she should back up remaining in a *sit* position.

The Word *Catch*

The word *catch* alerts Muffin to the fact that you are going to throw something to her and that you intend that she catch it. Having her catch a food reward can greatly reduce the time of training sessions and also save you steps in rewarding her. The quicker you praise or correct, the sooner your training will convey the intended message (see Chapter 4, Rule 8). Quickly tossing a food reward is as immediate as you can get.

Dogs vary greatly in their natural ability to catch things, but all dogs can be trained to do better than they would without training. Training involves throwing small pieces of food to Muffin. Command her to *down* about five feet (1.5 m) away from you, and toss a piece of food to her. Keep your tosses gentle, and initially aim at Muffin's mouth. When she succeeds in catching almost every one, angle your throws slightly to the side. Increase the challenge as Muffin improves. Build her catching ability slowly, always allowing her to catch more than she misses by adjusting the difficulty of your throws.

Typically, Muffin's attention will be on you when you are about to toss her a toy or a bite of food. Both are rewards that will arouse her interest and hold her attention. In this case, just say, "Catch!" and make the toss. Muffin will learn the word *catch* quickly because she will know that something enjoyable is coming her way—by air mail. If Muffin's attention is not on you when you want her to catch something, use her name first, followed by the word *catch*.

The *catch* command carries with it a certain trust that must never be broken. You ask her to catch only

those items that are completely and safely catchable. Her eyesight limits her ability to discern whether it's a rock or a piece of food. Build her trust in you by being as faithful to her as she is to you.

The Word *Eat*

The word *eat* refers to Muffin's natural ability to devour food. It is used in conjunction with *go* or *come* to direct her to eat, depending on your relative position. In Chapter 4, Rule 13, I explained how helpful it is to put Muffin through a short training session before you allow her to eat. The word *eat* is used to release Muffin from the training session to go eat. You should give the *eat* command as a reward only after she has

performed well. To train Muffin to understand the new word *eat*, simply say the command and run with her to her food. It is the easiest word you'll ever teach her!

The Word *Heel*

The *heel* command requires Muffin to travel along at your left side. In the *heel* position Muffin must always be aware of your speed, direction, and possible changes in either. Similarly, you should constantly be aware that she is with you and accentuate your style of walking to make it possible for her to maintain the heel position at all times. When you change the gait of the walk, making directional changes, or even stop completely,

If your dog is a good heeler, you'll find some competition in the obedience ring.

you should give Muffin a chance to sense that a change is coming. This is accomplished by slowing down slightly and signaling your dog to be ready to adjust accordingly. If you make a left turn, for example, you should slow down, make the turn, and accelerate slowly to your normal speed. If you don't slow down, you might find yourself tripping over your loyal and honorable companion. Before coming to a complete stop, you should gradually slow down and then stop. On stopping, Muffin should assume a *sit* position directly at your side.

If you are serious about teaching Muffin to heel, I would suggest that you seek professional help in your vicinity. Dog trainers generally specialize in this area and spend their whole lives helping people to train their dogs. Obedience training classes cover heeling, staying, jump-

ing, retrieving, sitting, and lying down. For training purposes, the classes present many advantages. You will have the guidance of a professional trainer, your commitment will force you to take your dog out at least once a week, and the school will have distractions that you don't usually have at home. The distractions usually consist of other people and dogs. You can be sure that when Muffin learns in spite of all the distractions, she will be able to carry out your commands when you and she come home. You'll like the trainer and the people you meet in the classes, since you all have an interest in common—your love of dogs.

Though almost all of the dogs at obedience schools are purebreds, dogs of mixed breeds are welcome. The only advantage that the purebreds have over the mixed breeds is in being qualified to compete in American Kennel Club sanctioned dog shows. Mixed breeds have the advantage of inheriting instincts from several different breeds. This makes them more likely to adapt to a wider range of training. If you'd rather not seek an obedience training class, the area of heeling has been covered well by many good authors in the field.

A dog that knows how to heel commands much respect in the community and is able to go almost anywhere. People will love your dog because they see few that are so well behaved and under control. A mugger would think twice before approaching a woman with a dog heeling at her side. Why should the mugger take a chance when the dog obviously has been well trained! If you train Muffin to heel, you will take her out more often and go to more places. Your life and your dog's life will be enriched because of it.

The Word *Jump*

The word *up* (see Chapter 9) directs Muffin to attain something at a higher level and to stay there. The word *jump* refers to your dog's springing or leaping. Use the word *up* if you don't care how Muffin attains the higher level; use the words *jump up* if you want her to leap up on something and stay there, rather than crawling up or walking up; and use the word *jump* when you require Muffin to leap over an object and return to the same level.

You can teach Muffin to jump by placing a stick on top of blocks at about half her height. Start by positioning it in a doorway or narrow passageway. Stay on one side, and command her into a *sit* position on the other side. Then give the command, "Muffin, come, jump it," as you back away from the stick. If you haven't placed the stick too high, it will be natural for her to jump over it to come to you. Continue to raise the height of the stick, and she will learn to jump higher and higher. A healthy dog should be able to jump over things that are

at least one-and-a-half times her shoulder height.

Once Muffin has learned to jump proficiently in the restricted doorway or passageway, place the stick and blocks in an open area. Then start all over again with the stick at lower levels. Teach Muffin to jump over various objects—a large cushion, a chair on its side, even kid sister Susie.

Later you can train your dog to respond to the command, "Muffin, go, jump it." Always be sure to use the full command—her name, the major directive go or come, and the words jump it. Also be sure to give Muffin praise after each success. A food reward is very helpful when the little lady's modesty gets the best of her and she has second thoughts about becoming the neighborhood's favorite!

Tundra responding enthusiastically to the command jump.

The Word *Pull*

The command *pull* requests Muffin to tug or drag something. She probably does this already when she plays with a sock or toy. Linking the word to the tugging action will further enhance your dog's versatility. She will not only know how to nose or push, she will know how to pull. When you ask Muffin to retrieve an object that is too heavy or too large for her to carry, she might be able to grab it and pull it to you. You can even give her a dresser drawer for her toys that she can pull out or push closed. Tie a rope to a lever-type door handle, and she can exit the room by pulling on the rope. Even if it's for demonstration purposes, you might find it fun to ask Muffin to go over to Aunt Gertie and pull her to you by her sleeve.

To teach the proper response to the *pull* command, find a toy or a sock that Muffin will hold on to and not let you take away easily. Pull hard as she pulls, and repeat the word *pull* each time. Many dogs will growl, so don't be alarmed. It's usually a friendly growl they enjoy making while playing. Try the play session using a 2-foot (.6 m) piece of soft rope. Tie several knots in the rope to help her to grip it. Once you are successful in getting her to pull on it, attach the rope to any article that you might want her to pull. Over several training sessions slowly reduce the length of the rope by cutting it, until the rope no longer exists, and she pulls on the article itself.

Avoid pulling with Muffin if she tends to be aggressive with people and other dogs. Pulling with you could encourage her to compete for the pack leader job. If you've been using it to exercise her, switch to an exercise such as jogging or retrieving a ball. These activities show Muffin that you're in control. Finally, if Muffin is still a puppy, put off training her to pull until she matures a bit. Puppies' teeth can be damaged by pulling too strenuously.

The Words *Upstairs* and *Downstairs*

If you live in a house with a staircase, you may find it worthwhile to teach Muffin the words *upstairs* and *downstairs*. Once taught, dogs can

readily associate the command with steps found anywhere. If you are upstairs you may wish to call Muffin from downstairs, or if you are downstairs you may wish to call her from upstairs. You may want to send her to deliver something to someone who is either upstairs or downstairs. If your friends are touring your home and Muffin has caused a pileup at the stairs, a quick command can allow the traffic to continue moving. Your life will benefit from her new knowledge, and her life will be less of a guessing game.

You will be combining two words from Muffin's existing vocabulary with the word *stairs.* When *upstairs* is used, it will direct her to attain a higher level by way of the staircase. When *downstairs* is used, it will direct her to attain the lower level by way of the staircase. You'll find

she will make the transition easily. If you and Muffin spend a lot of time hiking, you might find it helpful to add the words *uphill* and *downhill* to her vocabulary.

To teach Muffin the word *stairs,* find a place where she has the option of going both upstairs and downstairs. If there are three levels in your house, the stairways are usually positioned over each other. Begin training between the stairs going up and those going down. Command Muffin to go upstairs. If she starts heading in the wrong direction, say, "No!" Call her to you to try again. If she selects the proper direction and climbs the steps, praise her and call her back by saying, "Muffin, come, downstairs." Reward her with a treat and continue the practice. If Muffin stops halfway up or down the steps because she knows you're holding treats, get sneaky yourself. Put a treat on each level above and below you before you select a command. That will get Muffin to run all the way up or down quickly. You should be in fairly good shape yourself after a session of this! Be sure to keep her from heading up or down the wrong stairway, and make sure you use the proper major directive.

With a little repetition and practice, Muffin will learn her new words. As in all the training you've done so far, strive for mastery by trying different staircases, being farther away as you give the command, and having her carry items up and down the stairs.

The Word *Stand*

The three major positions Muffin can assume are the *sit,* the *down,* and the *stand.* You have already learned about the *sit* and *down* commands in Chapter 8. In the *stand* position, Muffin's body is parallel to the floor, with her weight distributed equally on all four legs. As in the *sit* and *down* commands, once you give the *stand* command, Muffin should assume the position requested and remain motionless until you release her. Though you will not use it as often as you do the *sit* and *down* commands, you will find the *stand* command very helpful when you need it. It is convenient to *stand* Muffin if you want to groom or brush her. Often it will be

necessary to have her stand so that a trick can be learned and accomplished more easily. If she is your traveling companion on wet or muddy days, you can have her *stand* when making a brief stop, instead of her usual *sit.*

To teach Muffin to stand, have her sit facing you and give the command. Gently lift the rear end of your dog, positioning her in a *stand* and telling her to *stay.* Reward her with a treat, then tell her to *sit.* Repeat this exercise until the lifting takes only a few fingers under the belly to let her know what you want. Make a big fuss over her the first time that she does a *stand* without help from you. As with all the training you've done, your excitement means everything to her.

The Word *Take*

Take is a word that will assist you in Muffin's in-house delivery service. When the command is given, Muffin should grab the article you hand her and deliver it to the person you designate. Unlike the *bring* command, in which the person giving the command receives the delivery, *take* is always a delivery of an article to another person. Until now you've had to tell Muffin to hold the object and then send her to find the person, saying, "Go to Joey." The word take allows you to give the command in one quick sentence. Just say, "Go, take it to Joey," as you hand her the article.

The training involved to teach a delivery has been covered earlier in this chapter. Please refer to the training method used to teach Muffin to deliver an article to a particular family member, and apply the new terminology to it.

The Command *Watch It!*

The command *Watch it! is* a handy way of warning Muffin that she should be careful and move out of the way of danger. In general, dogs are very trusting animals. They have a hard time learning what they should be afraid of because often they don't get a second chance. They need to make only one mistake to lose their life or to get badly injured. That is why so many dogs are hit by cars. In a crowd Muffin can easily get stepped on or tripped over. She trusts that no one will harm her, and she's not aware of the fact that some people just won't see her. Muffin will learn from the first few parties that being under a table is a good spot for an observer of her kind.

The command *Watch it!* can be used as a warning and teaching device. When you hike through the woods with Muffin, she may stop in front of you to listen to a strange noise. Unless you are aware of her reaction, you and Muffin may collide. If you've noticed that she has stopped, you can also stop, but

make sure you don't give her the *go* command to remove her from your path. If you do, Muffin, hearing your command, might take off after the animal she was listening to and get lost, be injured, or attacked. The proper reaction in this situation is to give the command *Watch it!* with the right emphasis in your voice. Here you are warning Muffin to be more aware and keep out of your way. You should warn her if a car is approaching and quickly show her that the sidewalk is meant for safety. If you are shoveling dirt and Muffin is getting too inquisitive about the smells coming from this mysterious hole, yell, "Watch it!" This may scare her away from the hole. A shovel can do much damage to a curious nose.

Avoid stepping over Muffin when she is lying on the floor. If you do step over her, you will be teaching her not to move. She will learn that

The command "Watch it!" can save your curious dog from having its nose bitten by whatever lives in this hole.

you and others will always take pains not to step on her. By no means should you trample Muffin! Rather, teach her to get out of your way from the start. Then she'll also get out of other people's way. To train her to get out of the way, pretend that you don't see her and fake a light fall, yelling at her "Watch it!" Inform your house guests of the words to use in case Muffin gets in their way. House guests will generally bend down to her to pet her, or they'll speak baby talk to her to try to get her to move. Neither of these is a very effective way to correct her.

The training in this book is based on keeping things positive. Don't leave things on a negative note when giving Muffin warnings. Every time the *Watch it!* command is given, it should be followed with praise for the proper movement. Use *Watch it!* to train your dog to

be careful and aware. You'll receive the added benefit of having a dog that will not inconvenience your guests or your family.

As you can see, there are many directions that you can take with Muffin's twenty-word foundation. The future of her language is now up to you. Try to communicate with her as effectively as you can, and you and she will surely be winners.

Chapter 14
House-training – A Necessity

H ouse-training refers to teaching your dog what he's allowed to do inside versus what he's expected to do outside or in a specific place. Bladder and bowel control is the first and most important training for a dog. Other than a convalescent dog, it's unacceptable for people to live with a dog that doesn't respect their home.

This chapter is aimed at house-training a new dog to your home or introducing your dog to a newly acquired home. The chapter will also be helpful for readers who have dogs who are not presently respecting their abodes. Getting back to the basics for a while can correct your problem.

Already House-trained? Skip this Chapter!

If you have occasional house-training problems with your dog, Chapter 15 will help you resolve those, as well as a wide variety of other problems that you may be encountering.

It is difficult to cover each situation for every reader. House-training will be reviewed in detail, but be sure to allow for your situation and the progress your dog makes. Acclimating a puppy to a home is a several-month-long process and a big responsibility. Working with a newly adopted older dog that has good bladder control but needs the proper guidance about the house rules will be much easier. Regardless of your situation, it's essential that you take it slowly. The time you spend on training will lay the foundation for many years of enjoying your pet.

A good philosophy to adopt as you proceed in house-training your dog is that you restrict your pet until he or she can be trusted and given more freedom as it is earned. It's an influential time so proceed slowly and realize that each mistake will increase the likelihood of another. It's a simple concept: Increase or

Restrict your dog until he can be trusted.

consuming, it's the way you'll make the greatest progress in training. If you are training a new adult dog or your house-trained dog is moving with you to a new home, you'll probably need only a week to transfer its training to your new home. You'll need to be more careful watching a newly acquired dog since you don't know what its previous habits were. If you are dealing with a puppy, you'll have many months of watching the puppy carefully. Fortunately, this is a lot of fun.

You'll want to give your dog what I call "observed freedom." Restrict your dog to whatever room you are in by closing the door behind you. Use temporary barriers, such as chairs, boxes, a piece of plywood, or a child's gate to block exits to more open areas of your home, such as hallways. This will keep your dog within range of your watchful eye and allow you to make a correction should he or she make a mistake. Shifting more of your time into areas that have easy-to-clean floors is a wise move! Kitchens usually work well and turn out to be the center of a lot of family activity.

reduce your dog's freedom depending on his or her progress.

There are many different ways of going about house-training your dog. Everyone has such different situations, that you will have to adapt the following information to form your own game plan. As you're executing your plan, don't be afraid to experiment and shape it into the best system that works for you.

There are three basic situations that arise in house-training your dog—when you're at home, while you're sleeping, and when you leave your dog home alone.

When You Are Home

Although house-training your dog in your presence is the most time

Most of the work for house-training involves frequent walks outside. Generally speaking, every time the dog eats, drinks, wakes up from a nap, finishes chewing a rawhide, tires from a playing session, has gone a while without a walk, or looks at you cross-eyed, take him or her for a walk! Also, be aware of the sniffing that your dog does outside right before he relieves himself.

When you observe that behavior inside the house, you'll know when to walk him. Accompany your dog and praise him for relieving himself. You can even give your dog a biscuit after he performs to encourage him in the beginning days. Allow him to earn your trust and the eventual freedom it brings.

If you're house-training a puppy, catch his first attempt to scent your home in its confined area and save yourself a lot of time. If you catch your puppy in the act of urinating, make a humane correction by giving the puppy a squirt of water from the squirt bottle (see pg. 112) while yelling the word "No!" Then quickly scoop up the puppy in your arms and take him outside for a walk. Ideally, you should wait until the puppy urinates outside so that you can praise him and keep everything on a positive note. Your puppy will quickly learn that he gets yelled at and squirted with water when he relieves himself indoors, and praise and a possible treat when he does it outside. The puppy's choice is an easy one. If you have missed catching your puppy in the act of urinating indoors, don't squirt him. Grab your cleaning supplies and clean up the mess as you scold him. Then, take him out for a walk and praise him as he urinates outside.

If you are dealing with an older dog, the correction will vary a bit. If you catch your older dog in the act, again make the correction with a squirt of water from the squirt bottle while yelling the word "No!" Make

your dog sit facing the soiled area or snap a leash on him to control him. Clean up his mistake while you continue to yell at him. After you have cleaned up the mess, escort him outside for a walk and praise him when he does his duty outside. If you're having trouble encouraging your dog to relieve himself so that you can maintain a positive note, refer to the training involved in the command word *walk* found in Chapter 10.

You do face a major problem cleaning up your dog's mistakes. It's very important to clean up the area thoroughly and remove the scent of urine from the walls, carpet, or anything else your dog has scented. If you don't clean it up effectively, your dog will continue to

The squirt bottle can be an effective training tool.

smell those areas and constantly be tempted to refresh his fading odor. It is best to use a product specifically designed to clean and neutralize the scent. Your local pet store will have some good products for you.

If you are house-training a puppy, you will find that your new pet will take many naps during the day. The pup will go from having boundless energy to being exhausted. At these times, encourage your puppy to rest in the area you have selected to limit his freedom. This will restrict the puppy when he wakes up so that you can control where he relieves himself. It's important to monitor your puppy, so that you can take him for a walk before an "accident" occurs.

While You Are Sleeping

Initial house-training will restrict your dog to a small area while you sleep. This training is based on the instinctual fact that your dog doesn't want to soil where she sleeps. It'll be most effective if you help your dog avoid soiling this area. If that happens repeatedly, you may have continual problems with your dog in the future. Because of this, it is best to be close enough to your dog during training so that you can walk her should she awake and exhibit uneasiness or start to whine.

In addition to restricting your dog's movement, you need to monitor the amount of water she receives before bedtime. Offer your dog some water about three hours before bedtime and then move the water bowl out of her reach. You can offer your dog very small drinks throughout this three-hour period, but don't let her fill her tank. You'll want to loosen the three-hour time limit as your dog deserves it. For larger dogs, remember to close the lids on your toilets lest you encourage an unhealthy habit.

Everyone has different situations to work around while trying to restrict the dog at night. If you are working with an adult dog, confine her to a small room or use a leash or rope to tie her to a heavy piece of furniture. You should make quick progress with an adult dog. Limit her space at night and increase her freedom slowly as she earns it. When using a small room, place some boxes or furniture around the room to restrict her space. If you're using a leash or rope to limit your dog, start with a short length and increase it gradually. If you're dealing with housetraining a puppy, you need to take more extensive measures.

There are two good ways to restrict a puppy while you're sleeping. One way is to purchase a dog kennel approved for aircraft travel to fit the expected adult size of your dog. Since the size of the kennel may be too spacious at first, you'll have to reduce the interior's space by blocking off a portion with a box or board. Cover the floor of the kennel with several sheets of newspaper. Check the newspaper for mistakes every time you release your puppy from the kennel. You need to keep the kennel clean and odorless. If you see the newsprint rubbing off on a light-colored dog you might want to cover the newspaper with butchers' paper or brown grocery bags. Later on in the training, the door of the kennel may be removed or tied in an open position, and a rope may be used to allow your dog more freedom. Do this by tying the rope to the kennel and putting a snap hook on the other end. A variety of snap hooks can be purchased at any hardware store. Give your dog as much freedom as she deserves during the house-training by lengthening the rope. Your dog will learn to enjoy the kennel as her dog house, not her bathroom.

Another good way to restrict your puppy while you're sleeping is to make a confinement board. Purchase a 4 × 4-foot (1.2 × 1.2 m) sheet of quarter-inch Masonite or board and glue a handle in the center of the sheet. Tape down newspapers to the Masonite, tie a rope to the handle, and on the other end of the rope tie a snap hook. The length of rope can be gradually lengthened as your dog earns your trust. Like the kennel, you'll find the confinement board lightweight and portable.

Expect a new puppy to be scared and cry throughout the first couple of nights in her new environment. Be patient and do not lose your temper. If you do, you'll only give your puppy another reason to be scared. Your puppy will probably need several walks throughout the night. Know from the start that you might not get any sleep at all! Initially, instead of waiting for her to awaken and exhibit uneasiness, wake the eight-week-old puppy every three hours and take her for a walk. Over the next few weeks, slowly increase the time between walks. At ten weeks of age, most puppies can last five hours without relieving themselves. Although all breeds and dogs vary, by twelve weeks of age most puppies can last seven hours. If your pup is awakening you with whining before your alarm goes off, it's a good indication

that you have progressed too quickly with your training.

It's a good idea to awake the older dog once during its sleep for the first week. You want to establish the house rules clearly. That should be all you will need to do. When you awake your dog for a walk, snap a leash on her and escort her outside. If you're dealing with a young puppy, it's best to pick her up and carry her so that you reduce the chances of her making a mistake on the way out. Warning: Cradling a puppy up close at this time may put a damper on your sleep. Later you'll gain more trust in your puppy's control and be able to snap a leash on her to take her out.

If your dog is maintaining bladder control through the night, make the kennel or confinement board as comfortable as possible with an old blanket. A blanket is a good choice because it can be folded to fit the area and it is washable in case your dog does make a mistake. The more comfortable you make her sleeping accommodations, the more likely she is to sleep - and so are you! It's also a good idea to have several of the dog's chew toys near her. She'll chew on them instead of chewing on bedding or shredding newspaper.

If your dog is having persistent trouble with bladder control at night, check with your veterinarian for a possible urinary infection or other ailment. If it's not a medical problem, then you may be proceeding too quickly with the steps outlined in this chapter. Back up and take it more slowly. Also, analyze your own actions. Are you giving food or water too close to your dog's bedtime? Are you rushing your dog's last nightly walk? Are you ignoring her cries during the night?

If you find that your dog has made a mistake, it must be cleaned up immediately. Make a humane correction by either making her sit facing the soiled area or snapping a leash on to control her. Clean up her mistake while you scold her. After you have cleaned up the mess, take her outside for a walk and praise her when she does her duty. It is very important that you leave everything on a positive note.

Some dogs wake up earlier than their owners would like. Don't allow those dogs to sleep for the last three hours before you go to bed. Throw a ball for them or encourage them to chew on a chew toy. If you can give them some nightly exercise, such as a walk around the block, that will help, too. If you happen to be up for a walk yourself, you might try waking your dog up and giving her a quick walk to relieve herself. This might allow her—and you—to sleep in.

Leaving Your Dog Home Alone

Most people worry about their dogs when they are left alone. All of your house-training can be ruined when you are not in a position to watch your dog. How much trouble you'll have depends mainly on your accommodations and your schedule. You can imagine how tough it is to train a dog for an apartment on the thirty-fifth floor of a building in New York City compared to a house with a yard in the suburbs. You can have a lot of trouble with a dog left alone for twelve hours, compared to a dog that is left alone for only two.

If you have a fenced backyard, from which your dog can't escape, it's a good place to leave him when you're away during the day. If your backyard is not fenced, you'll need to find another way to keep your dog confined. Your local pet store sells invisible fence systems, tie downs, and pulley systems that can be run between trees. There are certain risks inherent with each of these systems. Your biggest concern, especially if your dog is small or elderly, is that other animals might enter your backyard and attack your dog. Another worry is that a dog can get tied up in its own rope or around a tree and struggle all day, possibly causing injury. Also, dogs have been stolen from yards. Be sure to have a reliable neighbor or friend monitor your dog, no matter which system you choose.

A continual problem with leaving your dog outside when you're away is the weather. Your dog needs to have a shelter that protects it from the elements. If possible, install a dog door so that your dog can get into the garage, laundry room, mud room, or other small portion of the house. The kennel can be used effectively here, too. Place it just inside the house at the dog door's portal. Your dog will love the comfort and safety of his kennel. If a dog door is not an option, a proper dog house will provide your dog with some protection. Buy a dog house that's well suited for the breed of your dog. A wide assortment of dog houses are available for wet, cold, hot, and other weather conditions.

Most dogs are afraid of lightning even if they're inside your house. Imagine how scary it must be for them if they're stuck outside in a storm. Make arrangements with a neighbor or friend to come and get your dog if a storm is imminent. Another option is to leave your dog inside on days when the forecast predicts stormy weather.

Make sure your dog has protection from the elements.

Make sure your dog has protection from the elements.

If you don't have a backyard, you'll have to explore other options for when you're away. Experiment with different ones until you find one that works for your dog and your particular situation. Perhaps a retired person would enjoy your dog's company while you're away from home, or ask friends if your dog could stay in their backyard. In either case, have a monetary arrangement with them and insist on helping with yard cleanup. Check your area for doggie day care centers, and pet sitters as well.

If you have to leave your dog at home while you're away, find an inside area in which you can confine it. Until you can trust your dog, a garage or basement works best, since there's usually less for the dog

to destroy. Most rooms that are uncarpeted, hardwood floors excepted, are easy to clean up. Wherever you choose, remove anything that you don't want to be damaged or items that might prove dangerous, such as chemicals, electrical cords, and building supplies. You'll also want to make the area comfortable for your dog and leave him plenty of toys to play with and chew on. Before you leave your dog in this area, it would be a good idea to acclimate him. Confine your dog to this area while you're around the house, so that you can correct any behavior you find improper. For instance, if your dog is scratching at the door and barking, you can open the door and squirt him with a squirt bottle (see pg. 112) while yelling, "No!" Close the door immediately after the correction and listen to your dog's activities for at least a minute. Then, if he's been good, reenter the area to give him a treat and praise. If you're leaving your dog for a long period of time, it would be ideal if you could come home at some point or have a friend or professional pet sitter come by to let him out. It's also wise to exercise him well before you confine him to this area. The more worn out your dog is, the better.

In some situations, there may be a need to paper train your dog. Paper training involves teaching him to defecate and urinate on a newspaper-covered area. Although your dog will quickly pick up on it, paper training should be your last option, used only when your time away from home exceeds the dog's bladder control. If you paper train him, you'll have a daily smelly mess to clean up. If you must resort to this method, pick an area that's uncarpeted and easy to clean. A convenient spot would be the floor of the shower stall in the bathroom. You eventually will train your dog to soil the paper in the shower stall where cleanup would be easiest.

The training has a "can't miss" strategy that most dogs quickly learn. It involves putting newspapers down on the entire floor of the room in which you are restricting your dog. Praise your dog as you roll up the newspapers that have been soiled. Clean the flooring, and put down some new newspapers. Over the next weeks, slowly reduce the size of the area being covered by the newspapers, continuing to praise your dog for using them. The key to this training is to reduce the area of the newspaper slowly, eventually leaving papers only in a small, suitable area. If your dog misses the newspaper, you're going too fast. The positioning of your dog's bedding, food dish, water dish, and toys can discourage him from using certain areas of the room for his bathroom duties.

Having a dog you can trust anywhere you go is essential. A dog with good manners can be taken anywhere without fear of embarrassment. Your dog's life will be enriched with the extra things he will experience, and both of you will be rewarded with each other's company. Although there are many different ways of going about house-training your dog, the general training concept is the same. Increase or reduce your dog's freedom depending on how much he has earned your trust.

Chapter 15
The Problem Child

This chapter covers the wide range of problems that a dog can get into and some of the remedies available to its owner. I have included it in this book not to discourage you by telling all the problems involved in owning a dog, but to help you keep problems from developing and to solve them if they do. Some dog owners do not observe problems as they begin to develop. They fail to give the proper guidance at the very time it would be most effective and easiest.

Such owners label their dog a Problem Child as a cover-up for their own neglect in giving the proper guidance. Bowser could be a great companion, but they don't give him a chance. Problem dogs eventually end up being put up for adoption at a local shelter. They may eventually be adopted or mercifully put to sleep. If they are adopted by people who don't know how to correct their behavior, the chances are high that they will be returned to the shelter.

It is not my intent to discourage you from getting a dog from a dog shelter. There are very few bad dogs at these shelters. Most of them are stray dogs that once had uncaring owners. Others are those that people leave behind when they move away. If you do get one, merely correct its bad behavior.

There are no easy or pat answers concerning a problem that Bowser has acquired. Each dog is different. A remedy that works with one dog often will not work with another. The important thing is to keep thinking and trying. Define the problem. Put yourself in Bowser's position to figure out why the problem exists. The answer to the problem will be an adjustment, a correction, or a preventive action. All the problems that a dog has developed can be resolved without cruel, inhumane punishment.

In your quest for reshaping Bowser's behavior, remember the rules discussed in Chapter 4. Your corrections must be made consistently every time Bowser violates a house rule, and the whole family must participate. The corrections must be as immediate as possible, and your voice should sound like

This Golden Retriever is ready for an adventure. Teach him to stay within certain boundaries, and he won't become a Wanderer.

you mean it! You should change the negative into a positive whenever possible. Finally, if all else fails, remove the temptation that is causing Bowser to be bad. Enable him to be good! If you and the other members of your family follow these basic rules, in most cases Bowser's behavior will start to improve almost at once.

Use of the Squirt Bottle

There are many methods you can use in correcting Bowser. Most people will use physical corrections, which can vary to a large degree in their intensities. In this book, I've suggested leash corrections and gently helping Bowser into certain physical positions. My concern is that if I encourage a physical correction, which can be invaluable in dog training, some readers will overdo it and abuse their dogs out of frustration. *Never hit your dog.* You want your dog to love you, not to fear you. The squirt bottle is a useful tool for humanely training your dog.

The use of the squirt bottle is the best method I have found to accomplish corrections. The method is humane and very effective from the dog's point of view. Ideally, you want to make a quick correction and leave things on a positive note. The squirt bottle enables you to do this with a single squirt. You also benefit from being able to make the correction from a distance.

Throughout this chapter, we will be utilizing a squirt bottle to make many of the corrections. You will want to yell the word command *no* in conjunction with every squirt that is given. It is also crucial that you praise your dog when he listens to you and stops the improper behavior.

You will find that there are many types of squirt bottles on the market. Buy several of these and keep them in the places where you usually correct Bowser. I prefer a short squirt bottle that, when filled with water, is still lightweight and easy to hang on my belt by the handle. Mark the squirt bottles "Water Only" to prevent someone in the house from filling them with some kind of cleaning product. Set your squirt bottles to shoot a stream of water, rather than a spray or a mist. Squirt guns work well, too. There are many types of squirt guns on the market. Although the high-powered squirt guns might be effective at a distance, they pose a danger to your dog if used at close range.

The Backyard Barker

The Backyard Barker is a dog who barks excessively, disturbing the peace of the neighborhood. Each dog barks for a reason or a combination of reasons. Bowser may bark out of fear or loneliness.

He may bark just to get attention or to assert himself when the neighbors' dogs begin to bark. Often he may bark because, unintentionally, his owner has taught him to bark.

A Backyard Barker needs to be analyzed to determine why he barks. Only then can the proper corrective course be taken and followed. The dog that barks out of fear should be permitted to socialize more with people and introduced to strange noises. Have a friend in disguise walk by at different distances. Teach Bowser the difference between a passerby on the front sidewalk and an intruder. Reward him for not barking at a passerby, and squirt him with a squirt bottle (see pg. 112) while yelling, "No!" if he does. Permit Bowser to bark only when the disguised friend begins to enter the territory not frequented by the common passerby. With this training he will give you advance warning of a visitor and may scare off those who would mean you or your property harm. The dog that is always barking fails in calling attention to a thief.

Often a dog that is by itself all day is just plain lonely. Here the introduction of another dog or pet could be the answer. Neighbors can often combine their dogs in one backyard during the day to solve the problem. The dogs will get good exercise, have fun, and—ideally—be much quieter. Dogs that seem to enjoy barking or "gossiping" with neighbor dogs can be broken of the habit by using squirt bottle corrective methods.

Dogs that bark for attention usually are unintentionally taught to bark by their owners. Some owners who hear their dog bark excessively, possibly disturbing the neighbors, will run outside and reward him in one way or another. These unintentional rewards can take the form of a food offering to keep Bowser quiet, a scratch on the head to calm him down, a chew toy, scolding in a high voice, or bringing Bowser inside the house so that he quits barking. You can see how the owners solve the problem temporarily, but have forgotten about the long-range consequences. From now on, all their little lord and master has to do is to bark if he wants food, attention, something to chew on, or maybe just to come inside.

There are many methods available to you to quiet Bowser if he becomes a Backyard Barker. I prefer simply to yell, "No!" and to wait for a few seconds of quiet before praising him for listening to me. If Bowser continues to bark, run over to him and squirt him with the squirt bottle while saying, "No!" Never call him to you and scold him. You don't want him to associate his coming to you as being something bad, or he will hesitate to come to you whenever you call him.

There are many products on the market that might be tried if your attempts at training fail. Among them are a variety of electric collars. Although I don't like the basic concept, some dogs require only a few corrections by the collar to stop their barking—much to the relief of the neighbors. You will also find collars that emit annoying sounds and sprays that will provide Bowser with a correction. Whichever devices you purchase, research their quality and available options, and don't be afraid to return a product if you are unhappy with it.

The Chewer

The Chewer is a dog that bites, tears, and crushes your personal possessions. The object of this chewing might be your tennis shoe, a piece of furniture, a small tree in your backyard, or even a wooden slat from your fence. Dogs destroy or damage inexpensive items as well as exhibiting their finer tastes by chewing on the more costly things. Often the problem will go unnoticed until an expensive item has been chewed or until you have to send your son to school wearing only half a shoe.

All dogs are Chewers to various degrees. It's instinct that gives Bowser the desire to chew, and he enjoys doing it. In the wild it is nature's way of helping the dog keep his teeth healthy and his jaws strong. When a young dog is growing up, this desire to chew is stronger during the period when his new teeth are coming in. When new teeth are surfacing there is a lot of discomfort that chewing seems to relieve, just as it does in human babies.

The solution to Bowser's chewing problem is not to stop him from chewing things, but rather to redirect his chewing to objects that he's allowed to chew. There are many good chew toys on the market. Purchase a variety of them, and find the chew toy that Bowser enjoys the most. Chew toys that last a year are economical, but they will fail to relieve your dog's need to chew unless they are used daily. You'll even find an assortment of safely prepared bones on the market. They will also give your dog much chewing enjoyment. I prefer the small beef-hide chew toys that Bowser will soften and eat in the course of twenty minutes. Don't worry if he swallows his chew toys. They shouldn't harm him. However, choking is possible, so it is best to supervise him. Keep a good quantity of chewing articles on hand and literally at Bowser's disposal, or he might look around for something on his own. The object of his affection might be more expensive to replace than chew toys or bones.

Some owners will have trouble only when they leave the Chewer at home by himself. In most cases the destruction occurs within thirty minutes of the owner's leaving. If this problem sounds familiar, try to fake your departure and watch from an outside window. Catching him in the act will help solve the behavior problem. Also, make the act of leaving and coming home less eventful in the future. Don't make a big deal about saying good-bye on leaving or greeting him on your return. You could even reduce your dog's anxiety by repeatedly going in and out of your house. You want Bowser to be bored with it.

Preventive methods should be followed until Bowser can tell the rights from the wrongs when it comes to indulging himself in the fine art of chewing. Walk around your house and look for trouble spots that might look delectable to Bowser. If you have a rocking chair for instance, you'll notice that the rockers are at a very comfortable chewing height. They will probably be the correct size for him to get into his mouth. This particular temptation—and others—may be removed temporarily, be watched closely when Bowser nears it, or be treated with a repellent. There are repellents on the market to discourage your dog from destroying valuable items, but you can save money by creating your own. Use items such as bitters, Tabasco sauce, or anything evil tasting. Make sure your homemade repellent is indeed distasteful to your dog and that it won't stain or otherwise damage whatever you put it on. A young tree in the backyard can be fitted with a metal collar or with aluminum foil along its base to protect the tree trunk.

Corrections should be made as soon as Bowser starts to lick or chew your Queen Anne table, your Guccis, or your next-door neighbor! Tell Bowser, "No!" as you squirt him with a squirt bottle. Verbally give him a hard time. Then hand him something he is allowed to chew on, and praise him as he chews. For practice purposes, widely spread out on the floor a combination of dog toys and inexpensive household items. The training is simple. Correct him if he touches any item that does not have his scent. Do this with a squirt of water from a squirt bottle while yelling the word, "No!" Gear your training to allow Bowser to grab only those items that have his scent on them. Because of this, establish the policy that new dog toys are always handed to him. It can be costly and dangerous to allow Bowser to make a decision as to what is his toy. If a forbidden item has been touched by him, you will need to remove it and place it in the sun for a few days. This will prevent Bowser from passing by it and thinking it is his, since his scent is on it. Once the item has sat in the sun, grab it and re-establish your scent by blowing a hot breath on it and rubbing it. Continue practicing this drill until you no longer have a problem, and be sure to leave plenty of chew toys out for your dog's enjoyment.

The Trash Examiner

The Trash Examiner is a dog that seems to be trying to get his doctorate in "garbology," the study of garbage. His studies include certain special electives such as the kitchen

"How can they throw away such wonderful stuff?"

trash. He especially enjoys doing his assignments when no one is around to interrupt him. That's when he does his best work! The Trash Examiner minors in redecorating. On a good night he is able to arrange your trash in a very gifted way about the house.

Bowser's motivation to be a Trash Examiner stems from the many rewards the field has to offer. Dogs enjoy strong odors, and trash usually has a good bouquet. Bowser is attracted to it because the smells get stronger and more intriguing as they get older and as he gets closer. When he starts to examine the trash closely, a buried treasure is uncovered that can be licked, eaten, or carried around the house in play. For the little work involved, the whole experience is thoroughly enjoyable for him.

Once Bowser has found out how much fun it is to examine the trash,

it can become a bad habit, difficult to break. Dogs' memories are short. Unless you catch Bowser in the act of tearing apart the garbage, scolding seems to fall short of getting the message across. If you come home and find your house redecorated with trash, it is essential that you at least try to get across to him that what he has done is bad. Put Bowser on a *sit-stay*. While you are cleaning up the mess, convey to him the general notion that you're mad as a cat in a bath and that you're not going to take it any more! *Never hit your dog.*

Once Bowser has violated the trash, you must condition him to stay away from it. Try to lure him into sniffing the trash in any way you can. You need to get sneaky and set him up five or six separate times before he has a chance to repeat the offense on his own. Attract him by topping off your full trash container with a nice steak bone or even leftovers from dinner. Hide and watch what happens. When he comes up to sniff it, run toward him and squirt him with a squirt bottle while yelling "No!" By making your correction on the sniff, before the actual eating, you will send Bowser the message to avoid the trash completely. The sniff is his first step toward behaving badly. Your correction is not as effective once he has grabbed or eaten the tempting food. He has already received a reward. Repeat this training until there is no longer a problem.

For those dogs that have been examining the trash for years, you will want to intensify this training. Pick a time when you will be occupying a certain room with Bowser for a longer period of time, like when you're watching a movie for example. Set up several trash cans topped off with tempting delights. This way you easily can make repeated corrections as he checks them out.

If your dog is disturbing the trash cans in the backyard, bait him once more. Put a small volunteer in the trash can (I know—phew!), close the lid, put something extremely good smelling on top, and then let Bowser into the yard. When he goes over to investigate, have the hidden helper scare the fur off him by jumping up and yelling. If it's the stored trash bags in the garage that are the victims, rig a clothesline around them with noisy cans to scare him or, even better, hide in the rafters with a bucket of water. It will all come down to who's the smarter, you or Bowser.

There are several products on the market that you might try if your attempts at training fail. These products have been designed to sit in the trash can and give humane, negative feedback to Bowser just when he's decided to be bad. In dog training this is the most effective time for a correction and these devices guard your trash can in your absence, doing the correcting for you. Whatever devices you purchase, don't be afraid to return the product if you are not happy with it.

If your attempts at training the Trash Examiner fail completely, then move your kitchen trash behind a closet door, barricade the trash cans in the backyard, and put the trash bags in the garage up off the floor, where he can't examine them.

The Body Climber

The Body Climber is a dog that assaults people by running toward them and jumping up on them with its front paws. Other than being just plain annoying, Bowser can strike fear into the hearts of his new victims, can injure older people and children, and can dampen the prospects of an evening on the town by ruining a formal or tux with his dirty paws. The typical times for the Body Climber to jump into action are when you arrive home, when you journey through the dog's backyard, or when visitors show up at the front door.

Bowser has many reasons for being a Body Climber. For him it's exciting and fun to have people around. He's curious about what his owner and visitors bring into the house. At the very least, people have good odors about them. These might be the scent of your visitors' pets that clings to their clothing or the smell of food that their clothes have absorbed in their kitchen before they left for your place. Bowser may also climb up on people just to gain their attention. After all, no one else in the room can appreciate just what it means to be a dog down by the floor and have all the nice humans up above neglect him. Besides, Bowser knows he's not too good at verbalizing his greeting in appropriate "humanese." What wrecks all your training is that the victims often reward him by petting him as they try to regain their composure and push him off onto the floor.

Teaching Bowser not to jump up on you or anyone else will be easy if everyone cooperates in correcting him in the proper way. Usually pushing down on his nose with both palms while saying, "No!" *is* sufficient. A squirt bottle works well, too. Just give him a squirt while yelling, "No!" as he starts to jump up. If these two ways don't work, continue to experiment. When Bowser jumps, try grabbing his paws and step

slightly toward him. He will be uncomfortably off-balanced and won't like it. If you continue to hold on to his paws for several seconds, he won't want you to capture them again either. A loud noise can be used to scare him at the proper time; try a cap gun or a couple of lids from pots. If Bowser is a large dog, raising a knee for him to run into makes it uncomfortable for him. One of these methods or a combination of them will work for you. Remember to pet him only when he has settled down and become a well-mannered dog.

Teaching Bowser not to climb up on visitors is a problem when visitors lack the knowledge and your permission to correct your dog. Get your usual visitors and close friends to help you by correcting Bowser's greeting every time they come over. When strangers are involved, watch your dog closely so that you can make a fast correction with the squirt bottle. If you explain to visitors that you're trying to teach your dog not to molest guests, I'm sure they'll understand it and be appreciative, unless your correction is mean.

The Wallflower

The Wallflower is a dog that is easily frightened by people, animals, noises, strange objects, and even his own shadow. He's uneasy when strangers come or when he has to leave his home environment.

The Wallflower's plight is because of his owner's neglect to introduce him to life at an early age. He is not socialized because he has lived a restricted life alone in the house or in the backyard. Being sheltered and protected leads him to distrust and fear unfamiliar people and things.

By their very nature, dogs are cautious of some things. This is desirable as long as they don't overdo it. If you round a corner with Bowser some night and meet a gigantic street sweeper with its noisy whirling brushes and flashing lights, would you label your dog a Wallflower if he gets a little upset?

If you believe you do have a Wallflower, and you have made it a point to introduce him to things since he was a pup, he may have a physical problem. Poor eyesight, for example, may deprive him of a clear and distinct view of things. If you suspect a physical problem, see a veterinarian. Some conditions are correctable, especially if they are caught early enough.

The remedy for the Wallflower is socialization. A puppy can be socialized more easily than an older dog. The older the dog, the more gradual its progress will be. It is best to start immediately with your puppy and introduce him to as many new things as possible. Familiarize the puppy with young children, other animals, and people with long hair, no hair, beards, hats, and so on. Acquaint your dog with elevators, automatic doors, traffic, and car trips. Allow it to experience loud noises at a distance and then

gradually get closer to them. Some of these noises might be factory whistles, sirens, guns, or marching bands. If there is a parade in your area, take advantage of the mixture of loud noises. Put your dog on a leash, and keep about three blocks from the parade as you walk around the perimeter. Slowly move closer to the parade route as your dog seems to adjust to the loud noises and feels less threatened.

Your pup should also get used to being handled, carried, and having its full body examined, including its teeth. The secret to all socialization is taking it slowly and assuring your pet that everything is fine.

The Hyperactive Hound

The Hyperactive Hound is a dog that is very high-strung. While some dogs are sleeping under a shade tree, Bowser bounds with energy as if he had just risen from a long winter's nap. When let into the house, he runs around very excited and out of control. He is an extremely happy dog and needs little to amuse himself.

A tendency to a high energy level is typical of certain breeds but can be found in all breeds. Hunting dogs are bred to endure a long pursuit. They benefit from possessing the energy and staying power needed on the hunt.

If Bowser is hyperactive, his stamina can be a great advantage in training him, since you will be able to work him longer. Most dogs should be worked for only ten minutes; after that they lose interest in training and begin to perform poorly on new material. Young puppies can be classified as Hyperactive Hounds, but generally they settle down as they mature.

There is no real cure for the Hyperactive Hound; its usually just a part of his physical and mental makeup. There are two things that you can do, though, if Bowser is truly hyperactive. One is to make sure that he gets plenty of exercise. Jog with him, run him back and forth between two people in a park, let him retrieve a ball or Frisbee over and over, or get your children to run with him in the backyard. Good exercise will have a temporary calming effect on him, and he'll act more civil and less crazy.

The second thing is to teach Bowser that he must be calm and well mannered in the house. Don't allow him to run in the house. When he does, tell him that he is *bad*, order him to *down,* and tell him that he is *good*. When you release him from the position, sound as unenthusiastic as possible, so that he doesn't get excited and repeat the offense. Praise him when he lies down on his own by telling him that he's *good*, and then go over to him and gently scratch him. This rewards him for being calm and teaches him that being calm can

also be enjoyable. As he gets older, the combination of your training and the settling-down effects of maturing will make a big difference, and your efforts in training him will be more rewarding.

Exercise can have a calming effect on the Hyperactive Hound.

The Thief

The Thief is a dog that will steal food from you when given a chance. He sees an opportunity and takes advantage of it. If you are called away from the dinner table to answer the phone or door, you may find that Bowser has struck in your absence and has left nothing for your poor, empty stomach. As if that were not enough, your cunning little bandit has also grabbed your favorite dessert, which you left near the edge of the kitchen counter. You can't blame Bowser if he lacks the willpower to resist temptations of this type without training. You

yelling, "No!" Your timing is crucial here. Make sure he is not able to grab the food. You don't want him to be rewarded! Set the Thief up a few times, and he'll soon get the message that stealing food is a most unacceptable thing to do. Repeat this until Bowser can ignore your food, then go to him and praise him for being so trustworthy.

The Grabber

The Grabber is a dog that exhibits roughness in taking food offered him by hand. He is so excited that he hurries his nip for the food with total disregard for his benefactor's fingers, hand, and arm. This happens because the owner failed to subdue the dog's overenthusiasm the first time he displayed it.

An extreme solution to the Grabber can be for you to wear heavy gloves for protection whenever handing Bowser food. This preventive action lacks much merit, though. It's tough to live one's life in gloves. The problem with the Grabber can be remedied with a little training. If Bowser is a Grabber, take dry dog food or another snack that Bowser likes. Place it in a dish so that both your hands are free. Hand feed one piece of food at a time, and have in your other hand the squirt bottle. If Bowser takes the food roughly, immediately squirt him while yelling, "No!" Tell him he's bad, and recover the offered food. It probably will be necessary to remove the food from

are the one at fault. Through your carelessness, you've permitted him to reward himself, and he couldn't pass up the opportunity.

To put an end to your Thief's larcenous habits, you can do one of two things: Never leave food temptations within Bowser's range, or teach Bowser never to touch food that is left unattended. I prefer the second option because of the convenience in being able to leave food out and because the training involved is so simple.

To train Bowser to resist these temptations, plan a situation in which he is left alone with the last few bites of your dinner on your plate. Make sure that the plate is left on the coffee table or anywhere within his range. Leave the room and watch him secretly. As he walks over to check out your dinner, correct the first sniff he takes. Squirt him with a squirt bottle while his mouth physically. If you do not remove it, the effectiveness of your correction will be reduced because of the reward Bowser receives in getting to keep it. Continue the feeding process until every piece of food is taken nicely. Repeat this training, having other family members or a neighbor feed him. You can also change the food item to something irresistible, such as a savory piece of leftover sirloin.

The Digger

As far as one's lawn is concerned, the Digger is a dog that should be required to register his paws as lethal weapons. He is so skilled at digging, he could sign up for house excavation jobs and upset a good deal of the labor market.

It is instinctive for dogs to dig. They've been doing it for a long time and for various reasons. In cold climates they can dig a hole to protect themselves from icy winds. In warm climates a hole can help them keep cool. In the wild, some dogs dig for safety and protection. Some dogs dig to hide bones and then dig again to recover them. Diggers seem to have an insatiable curiosity about what might exist another inch down. If Bowser's nails have a tendency to grow long, digging can be his own way of keeping them in check. If dogs always spent their time enlarging a gopher hole or a chipmunk hole, we humans could understand their

motivation. But the Digger just wants to dig and dig. I don't think he himself ever takes time out to determine his own motives!

If Bowser indicates that he has inherited a strong instinct for digging, I can make a few suggestions. You might clear the grass from a small well-defined area in a corner of your yard where he can feel free to dig to his heart's delight. Clearing off the grass keeps him from developing the idea that you are encouraging him to dig through grass. This misconception might lead him to leave the restricted area and apply his skills to the part of the lawn you'd like to keep free of mine holes.

You can start him by digging him some starter holes. You can be sure that your friend will be right there to help you, and you can lavish praise upon him as he slaves away. Make sure that the area you have chosen doesn't have any buried cables or waterlines. You wouldn't want him to damage them, or vice versa.

If Bowser happens to dig in the wrong area, put him in a *sit* position near the scene of the crime, point out the result of his waywardness, and scold him into shame. After the scolding, show him to the proper digging area, and, if you have sufficient devotion, take his paws in yours and help him start a new hole while praising him. This serves to show him that you disapprove of his digging in the lawn but approve of his doing it in his own little patch.

Repair any hole he has made in your lawn at once, filling it with some large rocks, to prevent his digging in the same hole. Cosmetic touchups can be made later. If you fill the hole with loose dirt, the chances of Bowser's redigging the hole are high because it is so easy to do. There are other preventive actions that you can take to keep Bowser from redigging the same hole. A commercially available repellent can be sprayed on tempting areas, or you can apply a homemade mixture of Tabasco sauce and bitters.

The Biter

The Biter is a dog that occasionally, or regularly, snaps at a person and may pierce the person's skin with its teeth. If Bowser is a Biter, he may be indiscriminate in his targets or show gourmet taste and bite only his favorite neighbors. He is not a dangerous dog who continues his attack, but usually limits himself to only one bite. Other than this sporadic biting urge, the Biter is a good dog and very loving.

The Biter's reasons for biting vary. There are few naturally mean dogs. The dogs that seem mean often had puppyhoods that taught them to be tough to survive, were trained to be vicious as they grew up, or suffer from a painful physical illness. Most Biters not only receive no correction for their biting, but are praised for it. Many household members tend to pet the Biter to calm him down and protect the victim from a repeat assault. This type of behavior defeats their purpose and encourages the Biter to make another attack in the future.

Dogs also bite out of fear. A lost dog that has been scared by honking traffic, chased out of a few yards, or pursued by a man with a big net can be dangerous if approached too quickly. Some dogs will bite a neighbor who has a beard or wears a certain hat because of a bad past encounter with a person who resembles the neighbor.

Certain breeds feel a strong need to protect. The Biter may give a very effective warning bite to guard his territory or his family. Children often lie about dog bites to gain sympathy. If a dog bites a child, it is often because the child pulled his hair, stepped on his paws, or otherwise mistreated him. Finally, there are the accidental Biters that unintentionally bite you while you are playing with them. Usually they are young dogs who still lack coordination and control or just forget their manners amidst all the fun they are having.

Make sure you correct the accidental Biters. Young dogs that bite accidentally while playing should be squirted with a squirt bottle while you yell "No!" Though the mistake was accidental, correcting them for it will make them more cautious in the future.

The more serious Biter has to be watched closely and corrected for any aggressive action he takes. The situation demands that you get tough and communicate to Bowser that a growl or aggressive barking is unacceptable behavior. Put him on a leash and use a training collar (see pg. 32) when you expect a visit from a friend he dislikes. Wait until he displays his aggression, then immediately make the leash correction while saying, "No!"

If Bowser is growling at everyone, avoid using a physical correction and instead squirt him with a squirt bottle while yelling "No!" Make sure you praise him for stopping the behavior, but be prepared to use the squirt bottle again for any growl you hear.

There are a few policies in your house that you need to change. Since Bowser has the misunderstanding that he is the boss and that he owns the house, change your furniture policy. Don't allow him up on the furniture anymore. If you see him up on your furniture, yell "Bad!" as you squirt him with a squirt bottle. Give the command, "Go," and praise him as he reaches the floor.

The Biter has usually been encouraged to protect your house. Change this policy by using the squirt bottle to discourage it. Correct him when he barks at noises in the house, when he barks at people walking by your house or yard, and when he barks when someone knocks at the door. Bowser needs to know that the behavior is no longer acceptable.

You will need to change your feeding policy, too. The Biter is usu-

ally allowed to eat whenever he likes, since food is left out for him in his bowl. It's time you take control of Bowser's eating. Prepare his meal as you prepare your family's meal. Since, in the pack, the lowest member eats last, duplicate this in your training. Place Bowser on a *down-stay* in the doorway while your family enjoys their meal. Once you have all finished, do a quick training session with him and feed him.

Try to encourage your family to control other aspects of the Biter's life. Up to now if Bowser wants to be petted, he noses under your arm. If he wants to play, he brings you a ball. It's no wonder he thinks he's the boss. Control these behaviors by not giving him what he wants. Tell Bowser, "No!" and wait for a few minutes until he's failed at his attempt. Then go to him and pet him or initiate a play session. I would even control where he sleeps by making it a different room each night. Take away any control he has over your family's life.

It's tough to have a play session with the Biter because dogs are quicker and more agile than we are. You don't want Bowser to feel dominant over you in any way. When you do play with him, make sure you play a game that you can always win. You don't want to chase him in the backyard in play unless he was dragging a long leash, for instance. In all retrieving games, add more control to the game by training Bowser to bring the article and sit until you grab it. At the end of the retrieving game, it is important for *you*—not your dog—to come away with the toy. In pulling games, you need to be strong enough to win and you need to use the squirt bottle to stop any growling (if your dog is not a Biter, playful barking is okay). If the squirt bottle is not dissuading his growling, stop the play session on the next growl and tell him that he's "bad." You might try pulling with him again later, and continue to train him that growling is unacceptable.

The best way to add control to the Biter's life is to train him. Make him listen to you! In particular, make him proficient at the *stay* command (see pg. 27). It's a command that makes him yield to you in a very submissive posture. Have all members of your family and guests take part in this training.

Food can be used effectively to retrain most dogs. If Bowser dislikes a certain neighbor, children, people who have an identifying characteristic such as a beard, hat, or cane, or just people in general, put Bowser's feeding in their hands. Split up Bowser's daily ration of food into sections and allow others to feed him. Have them hold the bowl as he eats. As he progresses, if it can be done safely, have your volunteers hand feed Bowser. Instruct them to keep their fingers together and their hands flat. In general, anything that he fears should be introduced to him. Have your volunteers wear beards, hats, ride up on skateboards, and so on. You'll find that with food, you can

desensitize Bowser to anything. You want your dog to drool when he hears the doorbell.

The Prizefighter

The Prizefighter is a dog that will take on any contender in the field, parking lot, or front yard. The Prizefighter's adversaries are limited to other dogs, most of which also possess the desire and readiness to fight. The battle involving a physical confrontation of biting and snarling persists until the weaker opponent yields submissively to the victor. Both dogs will usually have injuries from the match. These injuries are sometimes severe and occasionally fatal.

The primary reason the Prizefighter battles all new challengers is instinct. In the wild, dogs fight within their pack for leadership, and packs fight to determine ownership of territories. Though this is quite natural in the wild, fighting is unacceptable in today's domestic dog. Even though Bowser has an instinctive desire to fight, he should recognize you as the pack leader and respect your opinion on whether to confront an opponent.

Dogs also fight because they have their owner's approval. It's only natural that you will offer Bowser sympathy after a fight. This encourages him. He thinks that he has your approval to fight. Some owners actually enjoy watching their dogs in competition and praise them for it. I once heard two men argue about whose dog could beat up the other's! Owners like these suffer from the misconception that their dogs enjoy fighting. Actually, it's their own egos that they're hoping to feed through their dogs' fighting.

The Prizefighter needs guidance to break him of his fighting urge. If Bowser is a Prizefighter, go to a park on a Saturday afternoon and walk him around on his leash, using a training collar. Intentionally head toward people with leashed dogs. When Bowser suddenly moves toward another dog, make a firm leash correction while telling him, "No!" and place him into a *sit* position. Scold him and then continue to walk around the park, looking for another occasion to train him.

If an unleashed dog forces a fight by approaching you quickly, protect Bowser. The leash will hinder his ability to protect himself, especially if you hold onto it throughout the fight. It's a bad situation because you can't let go of the leash, and you can't hold it! That is why you need to stop the fight from occurring. Try to avoid the other dog. Yell at him to scare him off. Try to prevent the dogs from staring at each other; this is the initial aggressive act that usually starts the confrontation. If a fight does occur, give Bowser the best chance possible by dropping the leash. Yelling at Bowser or pulling on his leash inevitably gives his opponent a big advantage.

Coming between two fighting dogs or picking one up is extremely dangerous and not recommended. You can have both enraged dogs bite you. If possible, throw something between the two dogs or spray them both with a water hose. When the fight is over, scold your dog for his bad behavior. With a little work the Prizefighter can be taught not to fight. Remember, it's your obligation to avoid other dogs

"I coulda been a contender!"

Dog obedience classes will provide you with the environment you need to teach your Prizefighter to ignore other dogs.

when possible and be on the alert when strange dogs are around.

The Chaser

The Chaser is a dog that attempts to overtake cats, motorcycles, bikes, cars, and new mail carriers with what appears to be hostile intent. If Bowser is a Chaser, he exposes himself and others to many dangers. If he catches a cat, for instance, a fight will usually ensue, and casualties are likely. If he chases motorcycles or bikes, he can get caught under a wheel and cause serious injuries to both the rider and himself. Bowser's intense concentration can also cause him to neglect the danger of an approaching car. If he chases cars, the chances of his get-

ting hit are high. If he runs after the new mail carrier, you might be visiting Bowser in the pound, owe the carrier a new pair of pants, and get your junk mail a day later.

The Chaser is dangerous to others and to himself because of the lack of control the owner has over him. He enjoys the chase and the reaction he receives from the ones he pursues. Often the Chaser is just showing off his guarding instincts and needs a little guidance from his owner. Bowser might be exercising his instinct to chase prey, or he might have been unintentionally taught as a pup to be a Chaser. Your children could have played with him while riding bicycles. He chased them around and thought that this was acceptable behavior, since the children delighted in it.

There are two main things you can do to reform the Chaser. First, remove the opportunity for Bowser to chase by never leaving him unsupervised to roam freely. Second, it is important that you present the temptations of the chase to him several times and make the necessary corrections to change his behavior pattern.

If Bowser chases cars, the following plan can be effective. Buy or borrow from a young neighbor one of the high-powered, high-capacity squirt guns. Get a friend to drive you past Bowser. As Bowser chases the car, fire a stream of water at his body. Continue to make trips past Bowser until he decides not to chase you. When this happens, stop the car, praise him, reward him with something special, and end your training session. Over the next couple days, vary the type of car and repeat this process.

When Bowser is in his training collar, a quick yank on his leash will tell him that you don't approve of his chasing a passing car or anything else. With repetition, he'll realize that the leash prevents his pursuit and that you don't approve of his behavior. Try to set up situations that allow you to make the corrections. For instance, enlist a child in the area to run, skate, or ride a bike back and forth past your front yard. After you have broken him of the chasing habit when he is on his regular leash, you can use thinner and longer ropes as leashes in training him until you reach the point where you can trust him without any leash at all. If you see that Bowser's urge is coming back, just repeat the lesson.

The Backyard Surpriser

The Backyard Surpriser is the dog that uses your whole backyard as a private bathroom. If Bowser is the only one using the backyard, then there isn't a major problem. The problem develops when you start sharing the backyard with him. It's upsetting to step in one of his surprises. You can't fully enjoy your own backyard if you have to be on constant guard for hazardous material. You'll gradually tire of this and also of the fact that your dog's urine is burning large patches of grass in your lawn. The dog isn't to blame. He's only doing what comes naturally in the area you gave him.

If you have permitted Bowser to develop into a Backyard Surpriser and now want to correct him, begin confining his bathroom privileges to a definite portion of the yard. Teach him to respect the rest of the yard as he does your house. Establish the future location of the area by asking yourself these questions: Which areas of the yard are Bowser's favorite ones for such purposes? Where would the bathroom area be most inconspicuous? Which area would require the least amount of fencing material? If you already have a digging area, can it incorporate the bathroom area? Try to leave enough room inside this area so that Bowser will have room for both his "duties" and his play.

When you have decided on the area, fence it off and install a latched gate. This can be done fairly inexpensively, depending on the material you use. If you lack experience to do the job yourself, you'll find your local building supply store very informative and helpful. A height of four feet (1.2 m) works well even for large dogs. If Bowser jumps the fence, just tell him "No!" and put him back into the area. This enclosed area will be a convenience for you in the event you wish to confine Bowser to the area for any number of reasons: Your friend's dogs are visiting, or you are having a backyard picnic, painting the house, or watering the lawn.

The final step involves teaching Bowser to use the enclosed area. When he needs to relieve himself, take him to the bathroom area, supervise his performance, and praise him. Prop open the gate with a rock or a brick to prevent the wind from closing it accidentally. Leave him in the backyard. Every hour come outside and take him over into the area of the enclosure. Praise him for any duties he performs. Leave him in the dog area if you lack the time to run out hourly. He must not violate the main backyard. Survey the backyard for any mistakes he might make. If you find one, bring him over and scold him while you clean up the mess, just

as you did in housebreaking him. With just a little training, he will get the message. Test Bowser by letting him out in the morning and watching him secretly. If he runs back to the area on his own, you've succeeded! If he is sniffing around in an inappropriate area, quickly run out to him, scold him, and send or take him over into the proper area. In this case you will have to continue the training for a while.

The Occasional Accident-er

The Occasional Accident-er is a dog that makes a mistake on rare occasions, either defecating or urinating in the house. This could happen for any number of reasons, most of which turn out to be the owner's fault. If Bowser fails in this respect, it could be that you left him too long without a walk, or that he needed more time on the walk than you gave him. Maybe he rang the communication bell and nobody heard it. If he sleeps in your room at night and the door is closed, he had no way of getting to the communication bell to signal you. A poor diet or table scraps could have caused loose stools. Here Bowser couldn't control his elimination. If you gave him all the water he could drink before he went to bed, then you are to blame. Even if it's a physical problem or sickness, you are to blame to some degree for not recognizing that he was ill and needed medical attention.

With only a few exceptions, the Occasional Accident-er will continue in his undesirable role throughout his life. Resign yourself to this fact and expect it. All you can do is attempt to determine the cause each time Bowser makes a mistake and eliminate the cause in the future. This will minimize the frequency of the occurrences. Correct Bowser each time he has an accident, regardless of whose fault it is. This is necessary so that he understands that it's bad, and continues to strive to hold it until he absolutely can't any more. In almost all cases, Bowser is not at fault. Your scolding should be gauged accordingly.

The Macho Scenter

The Macho Scenter is a male dog that intentionally urinates in the house to leave his odor on the carpet, draperies, walls, plants, banister, and even the presents under the Christmas tree. Sometimes he'll release only a short spray at a time so that he can have plenty left to cover additional areas. I once saw a dog get so excited, he lifted his leg and scented his owner! The problem with the Macho Scenter is that everything in the house will soon become stained and smelly. Also, you can't trust him enough to take him anywhere. If you attempt to do so, you can immediately become a *persona non grata* and your little

friend a *canis non gratis,* if there is such a thing.

The motivating force behind the Macho Scenter is—again—instinct. It is his method of marking territories with his signature of ownership. Since dogs have a keen smelling ability and enjoy certain strong smells, urinating serves as a communication system among them. A male dog will cover another male's scent with his own to show dominance. When he approaches a female's scent, he wants to leave his own business card as a future greeting to her. He may even want to renew his previous scenting at intervals to make sure that it's fresh and show that he's still actively in charge.

Even though this scenting is instinctive, it's also instinctive for a dog to recognize that his owner, as pack leader, has a right to his or her own territory. For the dog to violate the interior of his owner's house is an act of aggression and a bid for control and dominance of his owner's territory. After all, he has his own territory outside, where he can pursue his instinctive needs to scent with his pack leader's wholehearted approval.

The best time to teach the Macho Scenter is before he turns into one. When you first introduce Bowser into the house, watch him carefully. Don't make a chore of it. Just keep him confined to certain areas with you until you can trust him. If you must leave the house, put him in the backyard or garage until you return. If you catch his first several attempts to scent the interior, he will learn that the behavior is unacceptable. When you catch him, use a humane correction by squirting him with a squirt bottle while yelling, "No!"

If Bowser already is a Macho Scenter, the road to correcting the problem is long and rough. As with the newly introduced dog, you must keep a close watch on him. If you catch him in the act, make a correction with the squirt bottle. Put him in a *sit-stay* facing the violated area and scold him. While he's sitting there, clean up his mistake. The major problem you face in breaking the Macho Scenter involves those places he has previously adorned. Bowser continues to smell those areas. These scents are a constant temptation for him to refresh his fading odor. Therefore, it is very important to clean up his mistake thoroughly and remove his applied scent from the walls, carpet, or anything else he might have scented. Your pet shop will have a variety of cleaning supplies that will work.

As I mentioned earlier, the problem is that your Macho Scenter is not recognizing you as pack leader, or your house as your territory. Bowser believes that he's the boss in the house. This is a serious situation that can lead to many other behavior problems. You need to reestablish that you are not only the pack leader, but that he is the lowest member in your pack! The training for controlling every aspect of Bowser's life is covered in the section titled, "The Biter" (see pg. 124). Facing the fact that the problem exists and taking these corrective measures will lead to a solution.

If, after all your efforts, Bowser continues to deposit scent, there are some products on the market that are designed to help you. Several brands of repellents are available for both inside and outside use. The inside repellent should be sprayed as a preventive to reduce Bowser's desire to scent. The product marketed for outside use, usually a powder impregnated with repelling oils, should be used around your prize rosebushes or anything else you'd like to protect.

The Bitch in Heat

A bitch in heat is a female dog in one of the phases of her reproductive cycle. It's a time of sexual receptivity in the female that provokes excitement in every canine Tom, Dick, and Harry in the neighborhood. The boys will persist in camping out on your doorstep and watering everything they can to convey the message of their ardent intents. They'll come knocking and scratching at your front door, and your house will be the best-guarded house on the block. Of course, you may prefer not to have all this protection at the price of feeling like a prisoner in your own home.

A problem at this time is an unwanted pregnancy within your household. It's a big responsibility to raise puppies. Besides, when you intend to breed your female, I'm sure that you'll want to pick the father-to-be with utmost discretion for the sake of maintaining and improving the breed.

Another problem at this time is that Gigi may unintentionally stain your belongings throughout the house. You can't put her in the backyard safely. Her four-legged Romeos can jump the fence, dig under it, or even chew through it. She will be just as anxious to meet her callers as they are to meet her. One thing you can do to save your furnishings is to get doggie diapers. They are available, and they work.

If you have to take Gigi outdoors, you may want to avoid risks by equipping her with her own little chastity belt! Birth control pills are available; consult your veterinarian. There are even antimating sprays on the market! Pills and belts aside, if you want to take her for a walk, avoid your own neighborhood if possible. You might consider jumping in the car with her and taking off somewhere you think her virtue won't be at stake. If you do, however, do not stray too far from the family car. The four-legged males can pop up when least expected, right out of the clear blue!

There are two other alternatives for protecting the bitch in heat. Use a public kennel during this period to protect Gigi from the possibility of a pregnancy and to save your home from possible damage. The disad-

vantages of using a public kennel are the costs involved and loss of the companionship of your dog for a couple of weeks. Make sure that you are honest with the kennels you approach so that they'll know that your dog is in heat. You can't hide the fact that she is, and some kennels don't have special areas to isolate her. If Gigi is not isolated, males boarded there may be harmed by their attempts to get at her.

The second alternative is to have Gigi spayed. (This operation cannot be performed when the dog is in a heat cycle.) Spaying means that her

"Nobody knows the troubles I've seen!"

they come avidly a-knocking at your door! I personally prefer this alternative. There are already too many homeless dogs. Having your dog spayed also seems to add to the basic convenience and enjoyment of owning a dog, and she will enjoy a healthier life.

Gigi's heat periods may be trying times for you. Don't show her that you're displeased with her, no matter how irritated you may be. It is not her fault that the laws of nature dictate all this. Don't scold her. Be glad that she is healthy and normal. Give her more love and attention than usual. After all, it is a trying time for her also.

If worse comes to worst and you catch Gigi and Romeo in the act, there is nothing you should do. Don't try to separate them; you might cause irreparable injury. Just be calm and let them separate themselves. If Gigi's choice of a mate is not to your liking or if you don't want her to have pups just yet, you can call your veterinarian and discuss your alternatives—the costs and the risks. He or she has rather simple procedures that will quickly relieve all your worries.

Minor Bad Habits

Until now this chapter has dealt with major problems that can be extremely disturbing to dog owners and disrupt their lives. Certain minor bad habits that dogs acquire can add anxiety to one's life. These habits will annoy some people and

Some people don't appreciate a dog's lick. You can train your dog to "kiss" only on command.

ovaries will be removed by means of an operation, and she will not be able to become pregnant. Once spaying is done, it is irreversible. She will no longer come into heat, and the males will treat her in a more sisterly way. No longer will not others. I mention them only because even the smallest irritating habits needn't be tolerated. You can decide if you want to break one of Gigi's bad habits. If you do, be persistent in correcting it.

If Gigi licks, cries, sniffs everybody, or puts her nose prints on your windows, and you'd rather she didn't, change her behavior. Make a correction every time you see her do something unacceptable with a squirt of the squirt bottle and yell, "No!"

Sometimes other steps need to be taken to correct unwanted behavior. If Gigi constantly begs, jumps up on the furniture, or sleeps on the bottom of the living room drapes, a three-phase method will work. Make the correction by saying, "No!", teach her the proper behavior by using a command, then praise her for carrying out your new command. In the above examples the command *Go!* can be given and enforced if necessary. With a little guidance and praise from you, your dog will catch on.

As you can see, there are many pitfalls that your dog may encounter if you aren't alert enough to see a problem developing. Catching a problem early in its development can save a lot of time and inconvenience. Some of the solutions examined in this chapter might fail to alleviate the problem you and your dog share. Nobody knows your dog as you do, so analyze the problem and what gave rise to it. Use your background and the best of your reasoning powers to determine a solution that will bring your dog's behavior into line.

Chapter 16
The Problem Parent

If you have persisted thus far in this book, it indicates that you are concerned about your dog and that you are not likely to be a Problem Parent. Unfortunately, many of us miss things that can put our dogs at risk.

Every possession you have requires an obligation to care for and protect your asset. Why should ownership of a dog be any different? Many Problem Parents ignore this responsibility. They fail to think of their dog as an asset and valuable friend. They do not foresee the problems and risks. Thus they endanger their dog's health and often cause themselves much anxiety. This chapter will cover those categories of dogs that suffer because of their parents. Avoid these dangers that are so often overlooked, and give your dog a better chance for a long and happy life.

Unidentified Dog

The Unidentified Dog is one that does not have proper identification. The lack of identification does not become a problem until a dog gets lost. What emotional experiences does a lost dog go through? No one knows. But I do know how anxious the owner usually becomes, how all of us who love dogs feel when we see a lost dog, and the time we spend and the trouble we go through in trying to locate the lost dog or owner. A lost child is a sad thing, but in one way the child is better off than a lost dog. The child is missed much sooner, more people are concerned about locating his or her parents, and the child can usually say at least something that helps reunite him or her with family.

There are various things you can do to keep your Buster from becoming a lost dog and both of you from going through anguishing moments. The simplest thing is to provide him with a tag containing his name, your name, your full address, and your phone number. Your dog's name is important. It will help a stranger gain his confidence and control him. Your phone number should include your area code in case you lose him while on a trip.

In addition to the name tag, a rabies tag is very helpful. Anyone seeing it knows right away that Buster is a family dog. Someone

Even your Rin Tin Tin should have an I.D. tag.

adopted by someone who falls in love with him. Don't be afraid to have him tattooed. The whole procedure is a rather simple one—a matter of tattooing a number on the upper inside of Buster's right hind leg. You can find veterinarians who will be glad to do it. In some localities various dog organizations will do it at minimal cost. They are usually associated with a national dog registry and will see that Buster is registered under your number. They will also tell you how to obtain a collar tag telling anyone finding him that he is tattooed and registered.

Having Buster tattooed will also alert any potential dognappers to the fact that trouble lies ahead if they steal Buster to resell him. The penalty for stealing dogs is high in most localities, but often the crime goes unpunished because the authorities need positive proof of ownership. Without the tattoo, it is your word against the thief's. An X-ray of the leg Buster broke last summer might be the only chance you have. A trick you might have taught Buster will mean next to nothing. The thief, on seeing it, can claim that he taught good old Buster to beg with his paws!

If you do happen to lose Buster, there are many things you can do. You can put ads in all the local papers immediately. State the name of your dog, his general description, and your phone number. I wouldn't state the area where you lost him. He might be miles away by the time the ad appears.

loved him enough to go to the trouble of providing him with immunization. He is safer to approach than a dog without a rabies tag. However, be sure to keep the rabies tag current. You can't expect the rabies centers to keep records forever. Attach the name tag and the rabies tag separately to Buster's collar. If he loses one, he may not lose the other.

The safest and surest way is to have Buster tattooed in addition to putting tags on his collar. The tattoo is a permanent identification mark. It cannot be removed in case he is stolen or is lost and then

Stating the area might prevent a reader from calling and troubling you although he has just seen a dog fitting Buster's description. Some people don't realize how far a dog can stray in a short time.

After placing the ad, call all the pounds in your locality. Call daily and make sure they keep the information on Buster on the top of their list. Daily contact will also indicate to them that you are concerned and that you remain concerned. In the meantime, search the areas where you think Buster might be. In unpopulated areas you might rent a bullhorn. If you lost him at a distance from your house, go there and search the general area. If you have no luck in finding him, try looking in the direction of home. Most dogs have some homing instinct. Chances are his searching brown eyes and his salivating jowls are on their way back to where his munchies are kept. While you are out searching, put up posters and signs everywhere. Have people call you with any information they have.

There are very few people who will help an untagged lost dog. You can surely understand why. It's hard enough to return a tagged dog. The untagged dog gives the appearance that even the owner doesn't care.

If you come across a stray dog that you are fairly certain is lost, then you are on the other side of the fence. You know that you should approach him carefully. You don't want to frighten him away,

and you don't want to end up in an emergency ward for rabies shots. You can show all the neighbors that you are a little braver if he appears to be a well-fed, well-groomed, family dog. First, look for any tags or tattoo. If there are none, watch the ads in the paper. If you can afford it, place an ad yourself. Some newspapers offer free ads for lost-and-found animals.

After a few days the best thing to do is to take the dog to a shelter. Some people think that this is like assigning him to death row. This is not true. Most shelters make an effort to find owners before they do away with strays or put them up for adoption. By the way, if there is a strong, mutual attachment between you and your newfound friend, you can tell the pound staff to put your name first on the list of adoptive parents.

The Pickup Rider

The Pickup Rider is a dog that rides in the back of a pickup truck. If you ask your veterinarian how many of these dogs he or she sees monthly or ask the owners of Pickup Riders if they've had any close calls, you'll be quickly convinced how dangerous it really is! The possibility of eye damage from hitting particles at 60 m.p.h. (96.5 k.p.h.) seems insignificant compared to the damage Buster faces if he falls out. It's not the four-foot (1.2 m) drop from the truck to the ground that matters, it's the speed

Allowing a dog to ride in the back of a pickup truck is not safe and not smart!

chances of survival are slim. Even if the dog survives the fall, he has nowhere to go to get out of the way of traffic, and the owner has no way of safely and quickly stopping to rescue him. If the owner has tied Buster in the back of the pickup with a long leash or rope, thinking that it will keep the dog from jumping out, he has made certain that his dog will be dragged along the highway if Buster jumps out. If the driver uses a leash short enough for the dog to just barely jump over the side, then he has sentenced Buster to a merciless hanging.

If your allow Buster to be a Pickup Rider in spite of the danger, then at least improve his chances of survival. Drive slowly and safely. Stay off busy streets, freeways, and interstates with minimum speed limits. Put some old carpeting down on the floor of the bed, so that he has traction. Tie Buster up with a short leash to the middle of the pickup's bed right behind the cab. This will prevent his reaching the side walls of the bed. Buster's traveling kennel may also be used, but must be tied securely to the pickup's bed so that it doesn't slide around.

of your moving truck. Even at 20 m.p.h., it is impossible for Buster to land and stay on his feet. The Pickup Rider risks breaking his hips, legs, ribs, and skull as he tumbles. If that's not enough, he risks being run over by a car. The driver of the pickup often does not realize for some time that the dog is missing. If Buster lies injured on the road, he could be run over several times. If he can still walk, there's a good chance that he will leave the scene and will get lost and disoriented.

The danger of the Pickup Rider can be further compounded. If Buster jumps from the back of the truck onto a busy freeway, his

The Wanderer

The Wanderer is a dog that is allowed to roam the neighborhood or countryside at will. Most of the time dogs become Wanderers because their owners do not restrict them to a certain area to relieve their physical needs and it's too much trouble for the owners to take them for a walk. Out of sheer laziness, some owners let their dog loose on the neighbors, their lawns, and young trees, hoping that Buster returns before sunset. If your dog is in this category, the exclamation "doggone" will take on new meaning for you.

There are many dangerous situations that Buster can encounter in the outside world, all because of his owner's poor judgment. Traffic heads the list, of course. Also on the list are fights with other dogs and cats, encounters with people who hate dogs, dog thieves, attacks by wild animals, farmers who shoot dogs, hunters' traps, being mistaken for game by hunters, poisons, and rotten food. Restricting Buster's freedom a bit won't make him unhappy. Rather, it will lengthen the happy life he can have with a devoted owner.

If Buster is a Wanderer, there are several things you can do to restrain his tendency to wander. Your best option is to have a fenced area. Landscaping can be used for aesthetic purposes and to provide shade.

Several companies sell and will install an "invisible fence." The fence consists of a wire that is buried. The dog wears a low-voltage shock collar and gets a slight shock if he starts to cross the buried wire. The dog is warned by an audible signal as he approaches the shock area. People who have

these systems are happy with them. Be warned that a dog can run past the border, enduring the pain, if the temptation is great enough. Longer-haired breeds might need a patch of fur trimmed so that the collar will be effective. Collar batteries will need to be checked occasionally, too. This system does not prevent other dogs from entering your yard, another potential problem.

As another option, people will set a cable between two trees to allow a dog to slide his lead along it. Make the line very taut and high enough not to decapitate good neighbors. They're pretty scarce! Then take a lightweight rope and tie a leash snap on one end (a snap that's usually called a dog harness clip at hardware stores) and a pulley on the other. This will allow him to slide the rope along the full length of the cable. You'll want to give him as much rope as possible. Start with approximately 15 feet

There is no question that it is safer to travel in a crate.

(4.6 m). Lengthen or shorten the rope, depending on whether or not Buster gets tangled in it.

Tie downs that screw into the ground are used to restrict a dog to the length of his tie-out cable. In both, the cable method and the tie down method, Buster's freedom is restricted, and he can become tangled, injured, or attacked.

A final alternative is to train your dog to stay within certain boundaries. As you can imagine, this requires a lot of training and policing, and is not practical for most people. Train Buster during the walks you give him daily, and he'll soon learn where these areas are. Use physical features of the land or landscape that can denote a clear boundary or line for him. A sidewalk, a stream, a road, or a row of trees will work well. Walk him on a long leash or rope around the inside of a restricted area, and correct him with the leash if he attempts to cross a boundary. Every time you take him for a walk, circle the inside of the area near the boundaries, and make the necessary corrections every time he attempts to cross them. Concentrate on the places where he is most likely to cross a boundary.

When Buster learns to respect all the boundaries, you can begin advanced training. Walk around the inside of a restricted area, but have him off the leash. When he tests out a boundary by crossing it, scold him, and continue the walk and the training. When he observes all the boundaries off the leash, it's time to let him walk by himself. Keep a watchful eye on him from the house initially, then only occasionally, to make sure that your trust is warranted. If it's not, resume the training. Your diligence will save your dog from a run-in with a car, and you from a run-in with a neighbor.

Junk Food Junkie

The Junk Food Junkie is a dog that receives table scraps and snack food items from the owner. Owners don't realize that this isn't the best thing for their dog. Even when they know better, they may not have sufficient willpower to resist the sad and hungry-looking eyes of their pet. As an owner, avoid feeding Buster any snack items that have sugar or salt in them. In the wild, dogs ate foods that were very low in sugar and salt and did not endanger their general health. Since dogs lack the ability to brush their teeth, sugar in the diet can harm them. Buster's teeth are important to his health. Bad teeth can cause him great pain and prevent him from getting the proper nutrition he needs to live a long life. If Buster has tartar and plaque on his teeth, it is a good idea to have the veterinarian scrape and clean them. These deposits will not only endanger the teeth, but will cause the gums around the teeth to recede, just as in humans.

It is important for you to watch Buster's diet closely so that he can enjoy good health. Either substitute pieces of meat for junk food or send Buster away while you are eating, so that you will not be tempted by his pleading eyes. If he is overweight, limit his food intake. Measure the food you give him nightly, and weigh him weekly to see if he has lost weight. There are also special dog foods on the market for dogs that need to watch their figures. The wild dog can survive for days without food, so don't worry if your finicky eater refuses to eat the food initially. If the diet dog food you've selected is dry, try adding water to moisten it a bit. If Buster's really hungry, he'll eat. The overweight dog is doomed to die before his time, since obesity brings on many disorders, such as hip problems and heart problems. It can cripple him with arthritis while he is still young. If you restrict his food intake, it is advisable to give him dog vitamins as a supplement.

If Buster is underweight, feed him twice a day. When you place the food in front of him you must teach him that it's time to get serious and eat it or lose it! Feed him in a restricted area that is free of distractions. Make the food as tempting as possible by adding vegetables and lean meat scraps from your own dinner. Canned dog food can be added to your dry food and used effectively to help him gain weight. It is tasty enough to make Buster want to eat more. If you are giving him only dry dog food at present, start by adding small amounts of canned dog food to his meals. Then increase the amount slowly; otherwise, the oils and greases in the richer food can cause Buster to have loose stools. Check his bowel movements for feedback. If they become loose and continue to be loose, cut back on the amount of canned dog food or switch to a brand that contains a higher proportion of meat chunks and a lower proportion of fat. A dirty dog dish can also cause loose stools and sickness. Keep Buster's dish clean. Don't arrive at the point where you are feeding him canned food only. He needs the rougher dry food to keep his teeth and gums healthy. Dog cookies can also be given after meals to increase weight and to clean his teeth and gums. Find the type of cookies that Buster likes best, and buy them in quantity to reduce your cost.

The Shaggy Dog

The Shaggy Dog sheds hair all over the house, the car, and everything else in sight. The typical owner is inclined to blame the dog, as if the dog loses hair intentionally! The fault actually lies with the owner, who doesn't take the time to groom the dog regularly.

If Buster has a hair problem, it can be greatly reduced if you brush him on a weekly basis. Brushing helps to remove the loose hair. The choice is yours whether to collect the loose hair while it is still on your

wise—like loose hair—work its way right into the midst of your life! Although regular baths are not necessary, an occasional bath will help free loose hair and may keep Buster off the Shaggy Dog list. If you lack the time to groom your dog, pet groomers offer a great alternative.

Unpedicured Pooch

The Unpedicured Pooch is a dog whose paw hair and nails need to be trimmed. Dogs vary greatly in how fast their nails and the hair on their paws grow. Their nails also vary in durability. Some dogs keep their nails worn down naturally through exercise. In domesticating and breeding dogs, people have altered the dogs' ability to take care of their own nails, as they did in the wild. It is the responsibility of the owner to watch his or her dogs' paws closely and see that the dog gets a pedicure when necessary.

The major reason dogs should have their nails trimmed regularly is to maintain the basic health of their paws. When nails are short, the cushion-like pads of the paws can properly lie flat on the ground and can evenly support the dog's weight on each leg, providing proper traction. If the nails are overgrown, the dog may try to chew them off and run the risk of getting an infected nail, or accidentally rip a nail off, causing severe bleeding. He may just lie around refusing to walk on his tender paws.

dog by brushing him or to gather it from all around your living quarters later. Twice a year, you will need to brush Buster daily to avoid hair pollution. This will be during the time when he drops his winter coat and when he sheds his summer coat. Don't be surprised if clumps of hair fall out at these times.

There are many advantages to brushing Buster beyond just removing hair pollution. It will remove old excess hair and allow new hair to grow in better and healthier. It also prevents large tangles and mats from forming. Mats, once permitted to develop, have to be cut out to remove them. If you brush Buster on a weekly basis, you will be able to detect ticks, fleas, cysts, skin diseases, ear infections, and other things that you might not otherwise notice until it is too late.

Since dogs don't rely on sweating to release body heat, all Buster needs is a good brushing to make his coat look shiny and healthy. It will remove the dirt that might other-

If Buster tends to be an Unpedicured Pooch, he will need occasional trimmings by you, your veterinarian, a dog grooming shop, or a friend. Having his paws pedicured will give him better traction on ice and uncarpeted surfaces. He will be less likely to scratch things with his paws. As you probably well know, people, furniture, and floors can suffer when he needs a pedicure.

It will be more convenient and less expensive if you learn to give Buster a pedicure yourself. Read the following explanation, and watch someone else trim his nails at least once before trying it yourself.

Find someone who is qualified to do it, and ask if you can watch. It's a simple procedure but demands the utmost care to avoid cutting the quick. The quick is the flesh lying inside the nail. It contains small blood vessels and is extremely sensitive. Depending on the severity of the cut, the quick may bleed one drop or very profusely. When you do the trimming yourself, be careful and proceed slowly. Buster will probably receive a better pedicure than he will receive from anyone else. You have something personal at stake and will take the time to be careful.

You will need a strong light source, a pair of rounded scissors, a dog nail clipper, a metal file, and some blood coagulant. Start by finding a location for making a mess. Roll your dog over on his back and shine a good light down on your work. Do one paw at a time. Cut the overgrown hair back

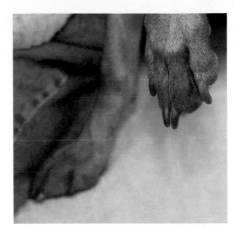

Examine the nail closely.

Carefully trim the nail. Avoid cutting into the quick—the tiny core of tissue that contains blood vessels and nerves.

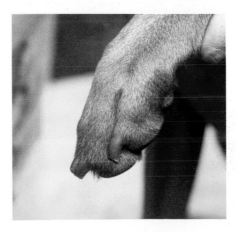

File off any rough edges.

145

to the level of Buster's pads, being careful not to cut the pad itself. Examine one nail at a time by holding it up toward the light source. If the nail is translucent or white, you'll be able to see the dark area containing blood inside the nail. Trim the nail back close to that spot. If it is a dark, opaque nail, you'll have to trim very slowly until you get close to the fleshy portion. Use the metal file to give a finishing touch and smooth out any rough spots that might scratch things.

The blood coagulant is necessary in case you slip and cause excess bleeding in using the nail clippers. Do not do a pedicure without it! In most pet stores you will find a product called KWIKSTOP, which is a styptic powder that is applied directly to the bleeding nail. The product is handy to have around for other minor emergencies.

The Toilet Drinker

The Toilet Drinker is a dog that drinks water out of the toilet bowl. This practice seems very convenient from the owner's point of view. The toilet always has water in it and is accessible to the dog as long as the seat is up. In most cases dogs develop this habit accidentally, when their owners do not provide them with water to quench their thirst.

Although allowing Buster to drink out of the toilet bowl may seem like a perfect solution, there are many potential dangers in the practice. Bacteria in the water could make Buster very ill. Cleaning chemical residue can also be harmful to your Toilet Drinker. If you and Buster visit a friend's house, there is the added chance that the toilet has a toilet freshener hanging inside the bowl or hidden from view inside the tank. These fresheners contain chemicals meant to deodorize and disinfect. Although deodorizing Buster from the inside out may not appear to be a bad idea, these chemicals should not be consumed by human or beast.

Even if you are always cautious, you are still endangering Buster's life unnecessarily. It's a bad practice that is unsanitary, unsafe, and tacky! Provide fresh water for Buster and correct him every time he drinks from the toilet. Yell at him briefly and run him over to the water bowl. After this bad habit is broken, leave the toilet seat and the cover down for extra protection.

In fact, if Buster is a toy breed or a puppy, he could tumble in head first and drown. To be on the safe side, always close the bathroom door and leave the seat in the down position.

I have discussed at length seven labels I attach to some dogs for which the dogs' owners are completely responsible. That is why I have called the owners Problem Parents. In most cases, the owners do not foresee that a problem is developing or that their negligence is creating a risk to their dogs' health and safety. If you are one of these Problem Parents in one or more of the cases listed, being aware of the problem is half the battle. I am certain that you love your dog and will act accordingly to avoid or correct any problem that exists.

Chapter 17
Doggie I.Q. Tests

This chapter will provide you with a variety of tests you can give your dog to help determine his or her natural abilities and inclinations. Although you won't come away with an actual score from the testing, you will come away knowing your dog better. Scoring all dogs on the same system would be invalid, as most dog owners have their own idea of what would make the perfect dog for them. This is especially the case if they are involved in one of the many dog sports or activities. The traits that make a good hunting dog, for example, will vary from the traits a good sled dog should possess.

If you already own a dog and feel you understand its personality and abilities, you can skip this chapter. However, if you want to have some fun getting to know your dog better, skip to the middle of this chapter and try some of these tests. They are quick and easy to do, and provide an interesting way to evaluate your dog.

Choosing a Dog

Are you looking for a new puppy or full-grown dog? Do you want more than just a pretty face? This chapter contains some shopping tips that will help.

There are a lot of advantages to testing. Primarily, you'll come away confident that you have selected the right dog. You will have matched your dog's natural traits with your anticipated needs. This matching will save you immeasurable time in future training and will enable you and your dog to attain a higher level of performance. The testing process will also give you a great head start toward creating that special bond with your new dog before you even hit your own front door. Starting out on the right paw will make a big difference in your life together.

This chapter assumes that you know the breed you want. If you don't, hit the books, attend some dog shows and, above all, get to know a breed's personality and compatibility with your lifestyle. Each breed will have different requirements for companionship, exercise, grooming, climate preferences, and medical attention. It might be difficult to invest several years of training and love in a dog

Pick a breed whose natural instincts match up with your anticipated needs.

when its breed has an average life span of only seven years. Certain breeds will outperform others in a specific dog sport or activity that you may have an interest in. A mixed-breed dog will have a variety of characteristics that may be just what you want. Take a little time to investigate!

If you have decided to go with a purebred puppy and know which breed you want, be familiar with what the dog should cost you. Of course this price will fluctuate depending on your breeder's evaluation of how each pup fits the standard—a description of the ideal dog of its breed. Breeders will be able to give you an idea of the price range between pet quality and show quality puppies. The difference in appearance between a pet quality and a show quality pup is

usually noticeable only to the trained eye.

If you can afford it, get your puppy from a reputable breeder. Better breeders work toward selectively eliminating the medical problems sometimes associated with a breed. A good breeder will guarantee your puppy's health and will give you a wealth of information about your dog and its care. Most pet stores, because of the public outcry against the use of puppy mills, try to get their dogs from good sources.

Whether you're getting your purebred or mixed breed dog from a breeder, animal shelter, pet store, or just a newspaper ad, take time to get some information. Who was the previous owner? How old is the dog? What is the medical history of the animal? If it is a mixed breed, what is the mix? Also, be sure the sales contract provides you with the option of having your veterinarian check out the dog.

Shopping strategies vary as much as the variety of dogs. You all know people who spend months buying a computer or a car, and others who buy on impulse. Even with the smartest shoppers, animals tend to fall into the impulse-buying category. Because of this, the tips for finding the right dog have been divided into two sections. The next section will describe some quick shopping tips that'll help you come away with a good dog. Continuing, there is a section written for the very committed, or you might say, a group of shoppers that some non-doggy people think should be committed!

Quick Shopping Tips

First impressions, whether of people or dogs, mean a lot. You can learn volumes about your pup in your initial evaluation. Some dogs will run over and jump on you. Others will approach you slowly, check you out, and accept you. Only occasionally will a dog be frightened and unwilling to come near. People tend to like a friendly dog that is very accepting, but there's a lot to be said for the dog that's a bit cautious at first and then becomes friendly. Be concerned about a dog that is

overly cautious or scared to come near you.

There are many advantages to selecting your dog from a litter of puppies. One advantage is that you need only to find the puppy that outperforms its littermates in the areas of your anticipated needs. Another advantage is that you get the opportunity to see how the puppies interact with each other. Watch for clues indicating pack order. There will usually be a dominant female and male. A dog may become the leader because of aggressiveness, intelligence, strength, or size. By watching, you will pick up many signs of each puppy's personality. Note intelligence in the way one puppy wrestles with another or plays with a toy. If you watch for them, you may see stalking, herding, and retrieving instincts. If the puppies' playing gets

Certain breeds excel in obedience competition.

Is the puppy trusting or scared when lifted?

and the Hand Towel Test. Most of the Ongoing Tests will provide you with useful information. They can be performed quickly anywhere.

Tips for the Very Committed

Although this approach to finding a dog is time-consuming and impractical for the average shopper, my goal is to give you the full range of testing material. Adjust the program to fit the time you have. Focus on tests that are most likely to reveal the traits you're looking for.

Many future dog owners have sports or activities they would like to enjoy with their dogs. If you fall into that category, you'll want to have a clear idea of the qualities you need so that you can find a dog with those natural inclinations. For instance, a puppy that shows a strong interest in sniffing everything is terrific if you are looking for a future tracking dog, but could prove to be a distraction if the dog is to be trained for obedience trials at dog shows.

Your first job is to find a reputable breeder, animal shelter, pet store manager, or owner looking for a new home for his dog. You'll generally encounter the most resistance at the animal shelters. They have policies that make it easy for the staff to say "No." Try appealing to the directors of these facilities. Fortunately, a growing number of

out of hand, you may witness playful growling suddenly change into an undesirable display of temper.

If you are with a litter of puppies, single out each one to see if it is disturbed by its removal from its littermates. Any overreaction should be noted. Jingle your car keys and toss them away from the group. Which pups are curious and independent enough to check out this new item?

Whether you are selecting a puppy or an adult dog, there are certain tests, starting on page 155, that you can try. Some of these tests will have to be adapted to fit your time and space limitations. Consider using all the Senses Tests, as they are quick to do and provide you with an idea of each dog's awareness. Of the Aptitude Tests, you'll want to do the Retrieving Test shelters are providing larger areas for visiting and playing with the dogs and many of your tests can be conducted there. You'll find that about half the pet stores will be very cooperative with your "test driving" their dogs. Some will even allow you to take a dog home for the weekend or allow you a store credit if the dog doesn't work out after a week. Whomever you approach, you'll need to visit with him or her and gain his or her confidence in what you're trying to do. The seller needs to understand the testing you would like to do in order to give you the freedom to do it. This person will have to place a lot of trust in you, and they will be inconvenienced. You don't want the owner or manager worrying that you are heading for the border with his or her Border Collie! You need to relieve the seller's anxiety about taking the pups or dogs out into the world. In all likelihood, you will be required to leave the entire purchase price as a deposit. Help your case and offer to do this early in your conversation. Point out that you will be spending a lot of time with your selected dog in the future and that all prospective owners should care enough to test their future companions!

Collect the following list of supplies for the job ahead:
- light leash
- gallon container of water, a dish for the dog and a cup for you
- notebook and pen
- dog treats
- folding chair
- old hand towel
- tennis ball
- box, ideally no taller than the dog and sturdy enough to support its weight
- noise-making devices, such as a squeaky toy, dog whistle, kazoo, or harmonica
- heavy book
- scents, such as cologne, roast beef, a fast food wrapper, or an onion
- different-colored collars if you are testing a litter of puppies

The testing procedure will differ slightly if you're getting a puppy from a breeder rather than an animal shelter, a pet store, or newspaper ads. If you are selecting a puppy, you'll want to visit the breeder weekly once the pups arrive. Make sure to have an agreement regarding your option on first or second choice. Occasional visits are fun, but don't fall in love with just one puppy. You'll need to be objective. The initial problem you'll face is that most of the puppies will look alike to you. At some appropriate point, ask the breeder to allow you to put different color collars on the available puppies. This will allow you to take good notes on their different behaviors. Try to schedule the testing as close to the litter's seventh-week birthday as possible. It is a perfect time for testing and for your new puppy to switch over to your "pack." If you're purchasing from a shelter, a pet store or a classified ad, there's no

Always use a collar and a leash to keep the dog safe.

reason to delay testing. A reputable seller, however, will not allow puppies to be taken out until they have had all their inoculations.

Your general game plan for testing puppies or full-grown dogs is the same. You'll take each dog out into the world separately and test it. Remain impartial and take good notes so that comparisons can be made. If you are able to take each dog out on several occasions, all the better. You don't necessarily want the dog that did well initially on the behavior tests. It is more important to find out the dog's ability to learn and adjust. Whatever your objective is in training your new dog, you'll want a dog that is able and eager to learn. The process is repeated until the field is narrowed and you've selected a dog.

Find a park that has playground equipment, protective fencing for the baseball diamond, a pond with waterfowl, or other interesting things that might be used in your testing. The next part of your trip will be a visit to the sidewalk in front of a busy grocery store where each dog will encounter automobiles, shopping carts, automatic doors, skateboards, bikes, and the scariest thing of them all—humans! You'll want to subject each dog to the same testing and environment so that you can make an accurate comparison. Be as consistent as possible.

There are many dangers out in the world. In public places, make sure the dog is always on a leash. You can allow each dog to drag a long leash for certain tests as long as it is within your ability to quickly control it. You need to put its safety first. Try to avoid other dogs. You don't want the dog in your trust to be attacked or pick up an infectious disease.

There are some general categories of testing that have been organized for you. This will save you time. Cover as much as you can with the time you have. Realize that a lot of the information you collect on the dogs won't be the result of a test, but will be accumulated by your just being with them. A good example is a car ride. Initially, most dogs are either worried or excited. You'll get to see how quickly each dog adjusts compared with the others. All will show different interests. One dog will enjoy looking out the window, another will insist on driving, and a third might show less than gourmet tastes by chewing on your seat covers! The pups will not be able to hide their different personalities.

It is unlikely you will complete all of the tests, so determine which ones better indicate the traits you desire and test in that order. You will not want to miss a crucial test because you run out of time. Make sure to add your own tests to the list and be flexible if an opportunity presents itself. For example, if you're looking for a future herding dog, you might interrupt your testing to head over to a flock of geese that just landed. It might prove interesting to see the dog's reaction.

Senses Tests

The tests below can be done quickly when you arrive at the park. These will check some of the important aspects of the dog's health. Unless you have a particular dog that performs poorly in a certain test, there is probably no reason to repeat these particular tests on your future trips. The tests aren't meant to replace your dog's first physical with your veterinarian, but to act as a starting point to give you some insight into the dog's reactions.

1. **Touch.** Gently scratch Fido as you perform a full body rub. Does he enjoy the scratching?

He should! It is an advantage later in training if he loves the scratching and thinks of it as a fine reward.

2. **Hearing.** Grab the various noise-making devices you have brought, wait for Fido to focus his attention on anything but you, and then try one of them. In addition to trying each one, honk the horn on your car, crumple a piece of paper, and try making some animal noises of your own. A dog should turn and locate most noises with interest, not fear.

3. **Eyesight.** Take a ball, a toy, or a stick and toss it 20 feet (6.1 m),

Your examination of the dog is no substitute for a visit to the veterinarian.

The barrier test is a great way to learn a lot about your dog.

Aptitude Tests

The following tests should be repeated on all future trips to the park. You want each dog to compete against not only the other dogs, but also against his own past performance. Remember, the park poses danger to the dog, so let him drag a light leash around so that you can quickly get control. Be sure that the area is securely fenced.

1. **Barrier.** The concept of this test is to encourage Fido to come to you when there is a barrier in the way of his direct route. The dog has to use its reasoning abilities and travel away from you to get around the barrier so that he can get to you. To set up the situation, find a chain-link fence or other barrier that allows you to keep eye contact with him. Playgrounds are good sources for this situation. Distract Fido by dropping several dog treats on the ground for him to eat. Make sure he faces away from the direction in which you're heading, and sneak over to the other side of the barrier. It is essential that the dog does not see the path you are taking. Once you get to the other side, wait until the treats are eaten, squat down, and encourage him to come to you. The barrier test is my favorite for indicating intelligence. If you have several different types of barriers in the park, test with them, too. Count

giving Fido a chance to see it fly and land. Each dog should follow the movement at least with his eyes. If there is anything in the park that is approximately one-half the dog's height, you can test his depth perception too. Just place the dog on the object and watch his reaction when he reaches the edge. Did he notice the drop or take a muzzle dive?

4. **Smelling.** Experiment with the different scents you brought and allow Fido to sniff them. Watch his reaction to each. Also, test him by spreading five small treats of food around a small area. How long does he take to locate them? Did he pursue the smell until he found all five? Remember to take into account the last time the dog ate. Unfortunately, a full stomach can throw off your results. If you don't know, ask when you return Fido.

to yourself so that you can approximate the time it takes each dog to complete the test.

2. **Retrieving.** Get down on the ground with Fido and throw a hand towel, squeaky toy, ball, stick, or other object several feet away. Note whether the object is ignored, chased, picked up, or retrieved. Be consistent in the amount of encouragement you give each dog so you can make a fair comparison.

3. **Box.** Take the sturdy box that you have brought and fold in the flaps of the lid. Place it in a soft grassy area and put Fido inside. Back away from the box as you encourage him to escape. Time his escape for your notes. Next, turn the box upside down and place him on top. For the dog's safety, the box should not be taller than his height, and strong enough to hold his weight. Note the ease or fear he shows in jumping off.

4. **Environment.** As you hike around the park with the pup, take full advantage of the terrain and man-made items. Climb up the hill, crawl through the concrete pipe in the playground, walk across the narrow bridge, and give him a drink from the water fountain. How does he react?

5. **Hand Towel.** Using the hand towel, tease the dog into engaging in a tug-of-war. If this test is being done on a puppy, be very careful because the puppy's

teeth can be damaged by strenuous pulling. Don't drag the puppy with the towel, but, rather, match the force the pup is applying. This test will give you an idea of the dog's competitiveness and aggression. Most people will prefer a dog that enjoys the playing but eventually shows signs of boredom, as opposed to the dog that won't quit. It would be great if the dog is talkative and growls playfully, but not viciously. Have you noticed a bad temper?

6. **Pulling.** Test the dog's ability to pull by putting it on a leash and tossing an article out an appropriate distance. You can vary this test with the level of encouragement you provide, the amount of resistance you provide on the leash, and the type of enticement you toss.

Some playground equipment, like the slide, is dangerous and should be avoided.

Does the dog get along with people of all ages?

Observation Tests

The tests below will give you a much-needed rest. Find a spot for your folding chair close to the action just outside a grocery store entrance, but out of everybody's way. Have the dog on a leash and just observe. You'll find that all dogs possess animal magnetism. Expect to see a positive change in each dog with every visit. Be aware that the black asphalt of the parking lot may be very hot. You can test the pavement with your hand and if it's hot, carry the dog to the cooler concrete sidewalk.

1. **Friendliness.** Is the dog friendly to the young and the old? How about to the person wearing a hat or walking with a cane? Was the dog unsure of the man with the beard?
2. **Awareness.** Let the dog's leash out a bit and see if it's aware of being in people's way. For the dog's safety, make sure you try this only with people who see him and won't step on or kick him accidentally.
3. **Anxiety.** Is the dog relaxed in this strange environment? His tail wag is a good indicator.

Ongoing Tests

These are tests that are more ongoing. They can be worked in throughout the other tests and repeated many times, if desired. Be observant and note the results of the following tests.

1. **Temporary Name.** Use a temporary name for all the dogs. This can even be the name you have selected for your future dog. By the end of all the testing the smarter dogs will respond to it. They will turn their heads to look at you or come to you immediately.
2. **Leash walking.** When the dog is on the leash, is he unhappy and fighting his restrictions?
3. **Vocalization.** Most people and trainers will discourage—or just not encourage—any vocalization. Appreciate a talking dog, and quell only unjustified barking or crying. There's a wide range of pleasing noises that a dog will make. You might note and encourage the dogs that try. Imitating the noises a dog makes will encourage most dogs to speak some more. It'll add to a dog's personality.
4. **Shade Appreciation.** If your weather has been warm and at least partly sunny, has the dog headed for the shade to lie down? A lot of dogs never figure it out, even on the hottest days. If the weather is conducive for the test, have the dog on leash and stand still on the border between the sun and the shade. Wait until he lies down and note his decision.

An intelligent dog will find a shady spot out of the hot sun.

Repeat this several times to be sure luck is not involved.

5. **Comfort.** Does the dog lie down in a way to maximize his comfort? The smarter dog tends to curl up to a tree root or wall so that he is supported. Try sitting on the ground and wait for him to lie down. Has he found your lap or at least rested his muzzle on you?

6. **Fear Response.** Is the dog spooked by everything? Check his response to your dropping a book on a concrete sidewalk. Allow him to watch and make sure you drop it flat on its cover so that it makes a loud thud.

7. **Curiosity.** A dog should be curious unless it feels insecure. Introduce Fido to something new and note his reaction (windup toy, balloon, stuffed animal).

8. **Abandonment.** The idea of this test is to pretend to leave the dog behind and watch his reaction. Try ducking behind a tree when he's distracted. You'll find that you can peek as long as you are still. A dog's eyesight is geared to movement. You can also try leaving him in the car and walking away. Make sure you don't have the windows completely down, because your new buddy may jump out and hurt himself. Good scores should go to the dogs who care where you are, but are calm.

9. **Trust.** While sitting on the ground, try holding the dog. Gently turn him over and cradle him. Does he struggle? He should trust you more every time you repeat the test.

For those of you who were selecting a new dog, you have separated the dogs from the pups. Your decision was a simple one. The dog that matched your personality and needs was apparent. You should be proud that you did not allow chance to enter into the selection process. You have not only started out your relationship with your dog on the right paw, you have given the dog a head start on its much-needed socialization and learning. In the future, continue spending time outside your local grocery store and visiting different parks. Make sure you introduce your dog early to field trials, backpacking, Frisbee catching, sled pulling, or other interests you may have.

Chapter 18
Parting Words

Don't allow yourself to be overwhelmed by all the material in this book. All it does is outline a good communication system that you can share with your dog and suggest adjustments in your behavior toward Fluffy so that you will be able to successfully guide and shape her behavior.

Some of you may be quite satisfied with your dog and her progress after completing the first stages of the training I've suggested. You may feel so satisfied that you will not complete the rest of the program. I encourage you to continue if you can find the time to do so. Those of you who do will find the work exceedingly rewarding, and your dog will relish the attention and training you give her.

Though the program seems idealistic, when it is properly followed it will make an obedient dog out of almost any canine. The reason for this is that the Twenty Magic Words are simple. This simplicity lies in the fact that only nine basic commands need to be taught to give you a most satisfying control over your dog at home and in public. Once these nine commands are mastered, they can be extended by teaching the secondary commands and the special commands, which will increase your ability to communicate with your dog. The ten additional words will make Fluffy a real pro. It will give her at least the equivalent of a bachelor's degree in the behavioral sciences from Poopoodo U!

The methods found in this book are based on principles of good training. Reward and encourage any behavior you wish to keep. Make it as easy as you can for your dog to succeed by progressing one small step at a time. Immediately correct any actions you deem undesirable, and, if possible, turn negatives into positives. Last, be aware of the mistakes you make in communicating with your dog or in training her. Don't dwell on them and fret over them. Just do your best not to repeat them the next time a similar situation arises.

The teaching of the Twenty Magic Words is easy if the methods I have presented are followed. In the initial training, select a place to hold lessons where there will be a

It's fun to watch a well-trained dog at work.

minimum of distraction. When Fluffy masters a command without distractions around her, train her to follow the same command in situations with a gradually increasing number of distractions.

Use food rewards as a training aid in introducing new material and as a form of payment for special deeds accomplished. Rewards such as verbal praise, petting, and playing supply sufficient positive reinforcement in routine situations.

For many centuries, dogs have been the victims of poor handling. Man's—and woman's—best friend has also been the subject of many incorrect notions. One such notion is that you must send your dog to a training school to have an obedient companion. Even if you do, Fluffy's achievements will depend on how

well you learn to give commands consistently. It is the same with the training techniques in this book. *The book itself will not train your dog; you have to do it.*

If your dog doesn't obey you, remember that it is your fault, not your dog's. Determine what you are doing wrong. People don't have dumb dogs as opposed to smart dogs. Almost all dogs have the potential to learn. It's just a question of your using the proper training methods. You can't blame owning a problem dog on bad luck. People create problem dogs by not providing the necessary guidance— the guidance that a dog, like a bright young child, needs.

The old adage "You can't teach an old dog new tricks" compares a person in a rut to an old dog on the false assumption that old dogs can't learn. I'm sure that this adage was not coined by a professional dog trainer. Although training is most effective when begun at an early age (seven weeks is not too soon), an old dog can easily be taught new lessons.

The dog of mixed breed has been said to be at a disadvantage compared with a purebred dog. Interbreeding is generally thought to be destructive by people who breed dogs. Undoubtedly this is true of the breeds these people are working with and the traits they are trying to develop. Centuries of work have gone into the careful, selective reproduction of most breeds. Indeed, society is fortunate to have such dedicated dog lovers. They breed dogs for specific functions. In each of these specific areas a particular purebred is usually superior to most mongrels. However, dogs of mixed breeds can often be just as trainable as—and sometimes more trainable than—particular purebreds because the mongrels may have inherited many instinctual traits found in their different ancestors' genes. They are thus more likely to adapt to a wider range of functions and will often learn faster. So don't worry if your dog is an old or mixed-breed dog.

Some people believe that it is unnatural and cruel to train a dog to do anything. This is untrue. It is instinctive for Fluffy to accept training, and she enjoys it. As a puppy she was trained in certain behaviors by her mother. If she had grown up

in the wild and joined a pack, she would have had a pack leader or older dogs around her. They would have imparted to her certain behaviors and training. Your training sessions, if carried out according to the advice I have given, will be a pleasure for Fluffy. She will look forward to them, especially if you hold them on a regular basis. Like humans, she loves attention.

Your dog wants to please you, her master, in every way she can. The only obstacle in her way is poor understanding. Fluffy will willingly

"I'm on hand to help you out."

do anything within her ability if she understands clearly what you want her to do. The Twenty Magic Words will make it possible for her to understand your commands. They stress good communication methods to increase her knowledge and understanding.

Good communication benefits your dog in many ways. Fluffy will understand more easily what you consider good and bad. Your wishes will be clearer to her, which will satisfy her goal of making you happy and make her life much easier in general. In addition to making your dog's life happier, it will provide her with added safety and improve her chances for a longer life. You are the one she loves and wants to be with. With good train-

ing she will get to spend more time with you, since you will be more inclined to welcome her company and take her with you more often.

The time, the attention, and the love you bestow upon your dog are very rewarding investments. Compared with the benefits, the expenses of owning a dog are minimal, both from a financial standpoint and with respect to the expenditure of your time.

There is much satisfaction in pursuing any hobby, but few hobbies can top that of training your dog. In other hobbies you are working with inanimate materials that do not react to you. You may end up with a painting, a piece of needlepoint, a musical score, or a rose garden that may be your pride and joy. But these achievements will not provide warm companionship on a cold night or fetch the paper in the morning! Like other hobbyists, you can display your handiwork and receive praise and admiration. People are always impressed by a dog that is obedient. They see so few.

In addition to having an enjoyable hobby, training your dog will provide you with therapeutic and psychological benefits. It's mentally healthy for you to have a dog that will always return your affection—a friend you can count on. The time you spend with your dog will provide a learning experience that can help you in understanding not only your dog, but other people and—most important—yourself. Finally, remember that the benefits of giving love, whether to your dog or to a fellow human being, are immeasurable. An additional dose of love in your life can only increase your happiness.

Everything is up to you now. Your success in teaching the language and using the training methods will assure your dog's success. Set your goals high and go after them. Allow your dog to be outstanding in his field and a credit to your work with him. Use the contents of this book as a guideline and refer to the book often. Don't allow it to be a book that sits on your shelf, never to be opened again!

Index

Abandonment, 160
Anxiety, 158
Aptitude testing, 156–157
Awareness, 158

"Back," 91–92
"Bad," 25–26
"Bark," 60–62
Barking, 112–114
Barrier testing, 156–157
Behavior problems,
    111–135
Bell, communicating with,
    7–11
Biting, 124–127
Body positions, 37–42
Box test, 157
"Bring," 52–53, 72

"Catch," 92–93
Chasing, 128–129
Chewing, 114–115
Clap, 75–76
Collars, 32
"Come," 31–34
    directed, 78–81
Comfort, 160
Commands:
    giving, 19–20
    releasing, 20
    secondary, 43–57
    special, 58–67
Communication bell, 7–11
Confusion, 15–16
Consistency, 13
Cooperation, family, 5–8
Crates, 104–105
Curiosity, 160

Dental care, 142
Digging, 123–124
Dinner, 21
Directed:
    "come," 78–81
    "go," 76–78
Directives, 27–36
Discipline, 16–19
Distractions, 15–16
"Down," 39–40
    hand signal, 81–84

Downstairs," 96–98
"Drop," 50–52, 71

"Eat," 93
Environment test, 157
Eyesight testing, 155–156

Family cooperation, 5–8,
    13–14
Fear response, 160
Fearful behavior,
    118–120
Feedback words, 25–26
Feeding, 142–143
Fighting, 126–128
Food:
    grabbing, 122–123
    as a motivator, 17
    stealing, 121–122
Friendliness, 158

Garbage, 115–117
"Get," 47–50
"Go," 30–31, 70–71
    directed, 76–78
"Good," 25
Grabbing food, 122–123
Grooming, 143–144

Hand signals, 75–84
Handclap, 75–76
Hearing testing, 155
Heat, 132–134
"Heel," 93–95
"Hold,"44–47, 69, 72
House training, 101–109,
    129–132
"Hurry," 65–66, 74
Hyperactivity, 120–121

Identification, 137–139

"Jump," 95
Jumping up, 117–118

Kennels, 104–105

Language, 1–3
Leash walking, 159
"Look," 59–60

Nails, trimming, 144–146
Names:
    learning, 23–24
    objects, 87
    people, 86
    places, 86–87
    temporary, 159
"No," 25–26, 70
Nose," 56–57, 71

Objects, names, 87
Observation:
    tests, 158
    tips, 151–15
"Okay," 65, 73
Ownership, problems,
    137–147

Patience, 14–15
Pedicures, 144–146
People, names, 86
Pickup trucks, riding,
    139–140
Places, names, 86–87
Play, 21–22
Positions, body, 37–42
Praise, 16–19
Problem behaviors,
    111–135
Progress record, 22
"Pull," 96
Pulling test, 157
Punishment, 11, 16–19,
    112

Questions, 90–91

Respect, 16
Retrieving, 157
Rules, training, 13–22

Scenting, 131–132
Secondary commands,
    43–57
Selecting a dog,
    149–160
Senses test, 155–156
Shade, 159
Shedding, 143–144
Shy behavior, 118–120

Signals, hand, 75–84
"Sit," 37
Smell testing, 156
Spaying, 133–134
Special commands,
    58–67
Spraying, 131–132
Squirt bottle, 112
"Stand," 98
"Stay," 27–30, 37–39
    hand signal, 84

Table scraps, 142–143
"Take," 98–99
Tattoos, 138
Temptations, 18,
    20–21
Testing, 149–160
Theft, 121–122
Timing, 19–22
Toilet:
    drinking, 146–147
    training, 101–109,
    129–132
Tone of voice, 14
Touch, testing, 155
Training:
    collars, 32
    plan, 6–7
    rules, 13–22
Trash, 115–117
Tricks, 88–89
Trucks, riding,
    139–140
Trust, 160
Tug-of-war, 157

"Up," 53–55, 73
"Upstairs," 96–98

Vocabulary, 1–3
Vocal sounds,
    89–90
Vocalization, 159
Voice tone, 14

"Walk," 62–64
Wandering dogs,
    140–142
"Watch it!" 99–100

Your dog can master a basic vocabulary of 20 words, and that's just the starting point for a home-based training program that will strengthen the bond between you and your best friend. With consistency, humane treatment, and cooperation from every member of your family, you can teach your dog basic commands such as *Come*, *Sit*, *Stay*, and *Down*. After your pet learns the first 20 words, you'll branch out into more complex commands that will tell your dog to bring you the newspaper, find your slippers, and go to bed on cue. As you follow each step in trainer Ted Baer's home schooling program for dogs, you'll be delighted at how willing your dog is to respond to your commands, and how easy it is to transform an unruly animal into a model canine citizen.